The
Holocaust

THIS IS A WELBECK BOOK

First published in 2015.
This edition published in 2020 by Welbeck
An imprint of the Welbeck Publishing Group
20 Mortimer Street
London W1T 3JW
10 9 8 7 6 5 4 3 2 1

Text & Design © Welbeck Publishing Group Ltd, 2015

ISBN 978 0 233 00613 0

Printed in Dubai

Editor: Alison Moss
Art Editor: Natasha Le Coultre
Layout Design: Luana Gobbo
Picture Research: Steve Behan
Production Manager: Marion Storz

THESE PAGES: Child survivors at Auschwitz-Birkenau on the day of the camp's liberation by the Red Army, 27 January 1945.

The Holocaust

Thomas Cussans

In association with Mémorial de la Shoah

WELBECK

Contents

OPPOSITE A Czechoslovakian Jewish woman and her daughter at the concentration camp at Kauntiz after liberation by the American 9th Army.

Foreword

Mémorial de la Shoah opened to the public fifteen years ago this year, in January 2005. It was created by the merger of the Mémorial du Martyr Juif Inconnu (Memorial to the Unknown Jewish Martyr) and the Centre de Documentation Juive Contemporaine (Contemporary Jewish Documentation Centre), which itself was created clandestinely nearly 80 years ago in 1943, to collect documents bearing witness to the persecution of Jews in France.

Since then our institution has grown to become the largest Holocaust documentation centre in Europe. Its mission is to preserve, study and transmit the history and memory of the Holocaust, educate young people and train teachers from all over the world to bridge the ever-increasing gap between the men and women who were contemporaries of the Holocaust, and those who did not experience this period of history, either themselves or through the memories of their parents.

As our President, Eric de Rothschild said – it is imperative to continue this knowledge down the generations in order to construct "a rampart against oblivion, against a rekindling of hatred and contempt for man".

This book continues our mission, reaching those who have yet, or may not get, the opportunity to visit Mémorial de la Shoah for themselves.

Mémorial de la Shoah, 2020

Introduction

It is one of the enduring paradoxes of the 20th century that a country, which had done so much to civilize the globe, simultaneously reduced it to an unprecedented barbarism.

Germany in 1933, the year Adolf Hitler achieved power, was a country seething with resentment. Its cultural legacy could scarcely be doubted. Its industrial potential was hardly less obvious. Yet in the aftermath of the First World War, almost every single one of its pretensions had been left in tatters. Its army had been forcibly disbanded, its economy ruined. Politically, it was fragmented, seemingly beyond repair.

In the midst of this chaos, the newly elected Hitler promised not merely to reverse the country's humiliations but also to reassert its historic destiny. This was to be the master race made startlingly real. The impact was sudden and heady, the consequences devastating.

Within 13 years, Hitler's self-proclaimed Thousand Year Reich had been shattered, the country prostrated, its cities ruined, its industries destroyed, its people left destitute. In the process, as the world was appalled to learn, a crime of unimaginable horror had been perpetrated. Six million people had been systematically eradicated in the name of an entirely mythical Aryan racial purity.

Hitler was hardly alone in his anti-Semitism. Yet no one, before or since, had attempted to exterminate an entire people. That said, no one had ever disposed the same industrial means to put their racial fantasies into practice, or the same absolute authority to order underlings to obey him.

The consequence was murder on a scale that remains numbing. The individual suffering can only be guessed at. Horror this great defies comprehension.

An understanding of the historical circumstances that fed the Holocaust remains the essential means of making sense of this otherwise inexplicable crime. It is no less the case that its impact is most vividly understood in individual stories. Stalin is said to have asserted with his characteristic mixture of cruelty and cynicism that one death is a tragedy, a million a statistic. Whether he did or not, it remains a remarkable insight: that deliberate death on this scale can never properly be understood. The numbers are simply too great. They overwhelm, they swamp, human imaginations. The suffering is too immense to be made sense of. As a consequence, the stories of the six million who died can only be sensed rather than known. The Nazis were assiduous in destroying traces of their crimes. What remains are no more than tantalizing hints of an unrelenting brutality: scraps of hastily scribbled diaries; a handful of illicitly taken photographs; the testimonies of the traumatized few who survived.

But if the details are blurred, the reality remains: the extermination of Europe's Jews for little better reason than that as supposed sub-humans – *Untermenschen* – their continued existence offended the Führer's vision of a future dominated by an Aryan master race.

The Holocaust sets out how the Third Reich evolved from a policy of the persecution of Germany's Jews to a precise decision to kill every single Jew in Europe. It looks at the organization of the killing centres and of the officially sanctioned hierarchy – the SS, its numerous offshoots, entire government departments, whole industries in fact, and a myriad of ordinary German citizens – that made possible these acts of terror.

It makes clear, too, that even if the Jews were Hitler's prime target, a series of other groups – any kind of "political opponent" as well as gypsies, homosexuals, Slavs and Christians – were no less his victims. It similarly highlights the use of slave labour in the Third Reich, vast numbers deliberately worked to death in order to fulfil an increasingly improbable vision of ultimate Nazi supremacy.

It is a book, richly illustrated, compellingly written, which offers a comprehensive view of the fate of a continent's innocents, one made more vivid still by the inclusion of a series of facsimiles of contemporary documents. It presents a gripping account of the single greatest act of mass murder the world has known.

OPPOSITE *Survivors and their families visit Auschwitz Museum during the 74th anniversary of the camp's liberation, 27 January 2019.*

Racial Purity: the Master Race and the *Untermenschen*

If confusion, chaos and opportunism were the hallmarks of Nazi rule, they were nonetheless underpinned by a series of constants. Chief among them was a conviction that, as Nordic Aryan peoples, the Germans constituted a superior race, physically, intellectually and morally. They were the *Übermenschen*, the master race. Inevitably, the necessary correlation to this belief was that all others were inferior, members of a number of sub-species or *Untermenschen*, literally "under-men".

In Nazi terms, they accounted for an alarmingly large part of the world's population: Asians, blacks, Slavs, gypsies and, above all, Jews, who in a characteristic example of Nazi logic were regarded not as members of a religious community but of a distinct race. By extension, the handicapped and the mentally disabled, including those of Aryan extraction, were similarly relegated to these sub-strata of the degenerate.

In arriving at these violent racial prejudices, the Nazis drew heavily on a series of mostly 19th-century, pseudo-scientific, racial doctrines intended to assert the supremacy of the world's white races, specifically of Aryan racial purity and fitness to rule. They were no less deeply influenced by the study of eugenics, another 19th-century development which maintained that "racial hygiene" – *Rassenhygiene* – could be attained only by the systematic elimination of "impure elements", chiefly by enforced sterilizations, to clear the way for the *Übermenschen*. The blind, the deaf and epileptics, as well as the more obviously disabled, were among those who were similarly persecuted, *Lebensunwertes Leben*. Likewise, homosexuals, unable to add to the Aryan race, were reviled. Above all, Nazi racial credos were fed by a European tradition of anti-Semitism that dated at least

from the Middle Ages even if the term itself was coined only in the 19th century.

That said, Nazi reactions to the Jews – "a parasitic race that feeds like a foul fungus on the cultures of healthy but ignorant peoples" in the words of Josef Goebbels – were coloured by the specific circumstances confronting Germany after the First World War. The Jews were denounced as not merely plotting a global conspiracy to undermine Western society – as exemplified by *The Protocols of the Elders of Zion*, a forged document produced in Russia in 1903 purporting to demonstrate Jewish plans for world domination and widely disseminated under the Nazis – but also they were held to have been responsible for Germany's humiliating defeat in the First World War. By the 1920s, Germany's Jews were the arch enemies, overly powerful, and they were blamed for inflation, unemployment, the Depression, white-slavery, prostitution and the ritual murders of Gentiles. They also achieved the remarkable distinction of being simultaneously

---

OPPOSITE Aryan womanhood at its most idealized and gleaming: fertile in every sense, industrious and dutiful, underpinning racial purity and national strength.

denounced as communists – Judeo-Bolsheviks – and as capitalists and profiteers.

If the Nazis were always slightly more ambivalent about just where the Slavs – whether Poles, Balts, Czechs, Croats or Russians – fitted into these racial hierarchies, Slavic inferiority was never disputed. Hitler himself called the Slavs "a mass of born slaves who feel the need of a master". Given that *Lebensraum*, "liferoom", a reference to those territories in eastern Europe (namely Poland and part of the USSR) to be settled by Aryan immigrants, was so consistent a Nazi goal, it necessarily followed that there could be no compunction about removing their existing inhabitants, however violently. The imperatives of the *Übermenschen* demanded nothing less. That said, the idea that Europe's Jews be murdered *en masse* in a Final Solution, or *Endlösung*, was one that evolved in response to the war in the East evolving. It was never a specific Nazi goal from the start.

Nazi views about racial purity may never have been less than confused, a hideous confection of prejudice and blood-lust directed at innocent victims, but they would prove deadly in ways even the most impassioned Nazi could scarcely have imagined.

OPPOSITE In 1938, ever more anti-Semitic, the Polish government declared that any Polish Jews outside the country would lose their citizenship unless they agreed to a series of arcane conditions. Fearful the 25,000 Polish Jews in Germany would become stateless, Hitler expelled them. The Polish government refused to admit them. For a number of weeks, they were forced into a hand-to-mouth existence in an increasingly squalid diplomatic no-man's-land.

Alfred Rosenberg (1893–1946)

Among a series of apologists who provided philosophical justifications for the Nazi's racial policies, Rosenberg, born in what today is Estonia, was the most notorious, a virulent anti-Semite, ferociously opposed to communism and convinced of the historic necessity for Germany to expand eastwards at the expense of the Jews, Slavs and communists. His 1930 book, *The Myth of the Twentieth Century*, a detailed and mostly incomprehensible anti-Semitic rant, sold over one million copies. He was among the foremost denouncers of "degenerate" art, by which he meant modernism, and a persistent advocate of "Positive Christianity", a confused attempt to reconcile Nazism, which was fundamentally atheist, with Christianity. He was executed as a war criminal following the Nuremberg Trials.

LEFT Alfred Rosenberg, intense and brooding, consistently dismissed by Hitler as "weak and lazy".

The Rise of Hitler:
from *Bierkeller* to Berlin

In the aftermath of the First World War, Adolf Hitler, approaching his thirties, was a blandly anonymous figure. He had served courageously in the German army, and continued working as an intelligence officer, monitoring the NSDAP that he later joined. He was also disaffected, with vague and violent dreams of future greatness at obvious odds with his obscurity. Within 15 years, he was Germany's head of state and had set in train a rule of brutality that would terrorize a continent.

ABOVE The Beer-hall Putsch of 8 and 9 November 1923 began with swaggering bravado and ended in humiliation.

The secret of Hitler's early success was improbable for so nondescript a figure: a gift for oratory that by turns was taunting, witty, abusive, seductive and ranting. To this, he added a growing love of power for its own sake and an instinctive taste for violence. At the same time, he possessed a kind of natural recklessness, a gambler's instinct tempered by an increasingly shrewd talent for political positioning.

Post-First World War Weimar Germany, newly democratic, fizzing with nationalist resentments over the lost war, politically chaotic, at times on the brink of civil war, and economically devastated, proved the ideal stage for Hitler's rabble-rousing. His own politics defied conventional categorizations, mixing elements of left- and right-wing policies more or less whimsically. Almost the only consistent features were violent opposition to communists and Jews, who in Hitler's mind were essentially interchangeable, and condemnation of the Versailles settlement, which had emasculated Germany's armed forces and imposed crippling financial reparations. The French military occupation of the Rhineland in 1923 was a similar source of bitter national shame.

It was on the back of these resentments that the Nazis emerged as a political force. Hitler, supported by one of many paramilitary forces active in the period, the brown-shirted SA or *Sturmabteilung* (meaning Storm Detachment), had become leader – Führer – of the Nazis – more formally the German Workers' National Socialist Party – in July 1921.

BELOW Hitler practised his speeches assiduously, striking poses in a mirror to perfect them. His command of his audiences became ever more precise.

Though he attracted the support of General Erich Ludendorff, Chief-of-Staff of the German Army in the First World War, who aimed to set up a new right-wing nationalist government, his political future seemed to have been decisively derailed in November 1923. What Hitler called the National Revolution began in a Munich beer-hall and ended in a pitched battle in the streets of the city that left 20 dead and Hitler in prison for a year. His release in December 1924 marked a new strategy. The goal now was not revolution so much as an embrace of democracy. Once installed in the German parliament, the Reichstag, the Nazis could then take over. German government was to be undermined from within.

On his release from prison, Hitler may have been able to reassert his control over a divided, squabbling Nazi party, but the elections of May 1928 saw the Nazis win a pitiful 2.6 per cent of the vote. Hitler, ever pragmatic, changed course. Left-wing policies were dumped; right-wing ones adopted. As a consequence, the Nazis began to attract support from conservatives, industrialists above all, fearful of communist agitation. Nazi electoral prospects were transformed. In the election of September 1930, they won 107 seats. As the impact of the Great Depression worsened – by 1931 unemployment reached six million – Hitler's nationalist rhetoric was ramped up. Further elections in July and November 1932 saw the Nazis emerge as the largest party in Germany. Hitler had moved centre-stage. Reluctantly, on January 30, 1933, after intensive lobbying on his behalf by financiers and industrialists appalled at the prospect of a left-wing coalition, the German president, General Paul von Hindenburg, appointed Hitler chancellor of Germany. It was an astonishing transformation.

OPPOSITE Hitler in best man-of-destiny pose next to the hardly more preposterous General Ludendorff in Munich in November 1923. Firebrand met doughty servant of the state. The result was still the routing of the "National Revolution".

ABOVE A wall of Hitler Youth and Brownshirts gaze adoringly at the Führer.

Mein Kampf

In Bavaria's Landsberg prison after the failed putsch of November 1923, Hitler wrote a book, *Mein Kampf (My Struggle)*. It has often been suggested that the book represented a kind of Nazi masterplan. In reality, it was little more than an incoherent, self-serving rant dressed up in pseudo-philosophical language. Hitler would later dismiss it as "fantasies from behind bars". If *Mein Kampf* has any significance beyond the fact that the money it made allowed Hitler a modest financial independence, it is that it made plain that there was never a coherent Nazi political goal beyond the pursuit of power for its own sake.

State Security:

Himmler's Empire of Terror

Nazi Germany was a state built on terror, terror directed against its own people as much as against its enemies. It was sustained by a vast edifice of secret policemen, informers, security agents and military forces operating outside any law and answerable to the most powerful man in Nazi Germany after Hitler, Heinrich Himmler, who was from 1929 head of the SS, and from 1936 head of all German security forces.

By 1944, the SS, or *Schutzstaffel* (Defence Corps), had become a major military force, with 40 divisions and almost one million men. Yet it had begun, in 1925, reformed from an earlier unit, as no more than a sub-unit of the SA, albeit charged as Hitler's personal bodyguard. It was the SA (led by Ernst Röhm) who were the original, strutting paramilitary face of the Nazis, swaggeringly terrorizing anyone they saw as enemies of the state. Jews and communists were their preferred victims. By the early thirties, the SA numbered three million.

Röhm's insistence after Hitler was made chancellor in 1933 that the SA become, in effect, the new German army under Röhm's command not only ensured bitter opposition from the (much smaller) army proper, but also guaranteed the hostility of the leading Nazis, fearful that Röhm's dominance could only come at their expense. Given that Röhm, aggressively homosexual (as was much of the leadership of the SA) and frequently drunk, was prone to

RIGHT Heinrich Himmler, the architect of terror, pictured in the mid-1930s. His thwarted ambitions to become a soldier in the pre-Nazi German army found a terrifying outlet in his leadership of the SS.

OPPOSITE There was little the SA enjoyed more than reinforcing their anti-Jewish propaganda by their bullying, sneering street presence.

making inflammatory statements about Hitler, it was easy to fake evidence that he was also planning to overthrow him.

As part of a general elimination of political rivals – the Night of the Long Knives – in mid-summer 1934, Hitler struck. Röhm and his senior SA colleagues were ordered to a Bavarian lakeside resort, Bad Wiessee. There at dawn on June 30 Hitler himself arrested him. Two days later, Röhm was executed. The remaining SA leadership was purged.

The way was cleared for Himmler, colourless, crankily obsessed with Nordic folklore, fanatically obsessed with Aryan racial purity and resolutely loyal to Hitler, to establish the most elaborate apparatus of state tyranny yet devised.

At its heart was the SS, intended as an élite, racially pure instrument of Nazi terror – all its members had to prove unadulterated Aryan descent from 1800. When Hitler appointed Himmler head of the SS – *Reichsführer-SS* – in 1929, it had no more than 290 members. By 1933, it had 33,000. In time, it would be directly responsible for all the principal instruments of the Holocaust: the *Einsatzgruppen* and all concentration, slave and death camps.

In addition to running the ordinary, uniformed police force, the *Ordnungspolizei* (or Orpo), in 1936 Himmler formed the *Kriminalpolizei* (or Kripo), which was merged with the Gestapo, founded by Goring in 1933, to form the *Sicherheitspolizei* (or SiPo). He was similarly responsible for an intelligence agency, the *Sicherheitsdienst* (or SD). In September 1939, a new department was formed under his direction, the *Reichssicherheitshauptamt*, the RSHA or Reich Main Security Office, which took overall responsibility for all arms of state security, including the SS. By the middle of the war, these security services employed over three million men, which, by coincidence, was almost exactly the number of German citizens arrested by them, an average of 15,000 a month. The Gestapo by now were not merely able to re-arrest those found not guilty in the courts but to execute them.

A vast agency of terror, by turns pettily bureaucratic, keeping precise records of false teeth and pocket watches recovered from its victims, and unimaginably savage, dedicated to the slaughter of millions, had been created.

The Gestapo

The reputation of the Gestapo, the *Geheime Staatspolizei* or Secret State Police, as the most ruthless arm of Nazi state terror was not undeserved. If by the end of the war there was little to distinguish it from the SS, it had nonetheless achieved its chilling aim. It was an organization whose primary goal was to strike fear in the hearts of its victims. It was given an almost completely free hand to act however it thought best. It expanded at an astonishing rate. At its height, it had 40 offices in Germany alone and employed 46,000.

RIGHT Czech suspects rounded up by the Gestapo in the Sudetenland to suffer an inevitably brutal fate after the Munich Agreement of 29 September 1938 allowed Hitler to annexe much of western Czechoslovakia.

Consolidation: the First Camps and the Nuremberg Laws

Eighteen months after Hitler was made Chancellor of Germany, the country had become a one-party state, Hitler its undisputed leader, his authority absolute. It was a process accompanied by a series of measures to cement Nazi rule: the outlawing of rival political parties; the first concentration camps; the active persecution of Jews; the glorification of Nazi rule through precisely staged rallies.

Chance played a surprisingly large part in the early years of Hitler's rule. Within a month of his becoming chancellor, the Reichstag, the German parliament, burned down. It was an event Hitler exploited instantly: "Now we'll show them! Anyone who stands in our way will be mown down."

The fire was almost certainly started by a disaffected Dutch ex-communist, Marinus van der Lubbe on 27 February 1933. Hitler, however, declared it the result of a communist plot to destabilize Germany. In the ensuing crisis, he imposed an Enabling Act on the Reichstag, which, meeting in a

VÖLKISCHER BEOBACHTER

former opera house, was effectively coerced into passing all executive powers to Hitler. At a stroke, Hitler had by-passed parliamentary control.

Beginning with the communists, all political parties, even those such as the Nationalists, who had supported Hitler's elevation to the Chancellorship, were declared illegal. Trade Unions were similarly banned. The logical consequence was that Hitler should then declare himself head of state (as well as head of the army). This he did in August 1934 when the elderly Hindenburg died. Opposition to the Nazis was brought to a sudden halt.

The previous year, the first major concentration camp, Dachau in Bavaria, had been opened. Though a series of other such camps followed, they were far from instruments of purely anti-Semitic repression. Rather, they were places of internment for "enemies of the state": profiteers, communists, pacifists, in short the usual roll-call of all those deemed "deviants" and "asocials".

To the extent that a coherent Nazi policy existed towards the Jewish question, it was that a combination of harassment and legal sanction would force the country's Jews to emigrate. The goal was not their extermination: it was to drive them away.

ABOVE RIGHT The 16 September 1935 edition of the Völkischer Beobachter *(German Observer), mouthpiece of the Nazi Party, announcing the Nuremberg Laws. From 1921, the paper was owned by Hitler personally. In 1923, Alfred Rosenberg became its editor.*

OPPOSITE A Jewish café on the day following Kristallnacht, *liberally daubed with anti-Jewish slogans. Approximately 7,500 Jewish businesses were attacked in this way and 267 synagogues burnt in acts of deliberate violence.*

Standing cells

One of the more extreme forms of punishment introduced at Dachau, subsequently extended to other Nazi camps, was the standing cell. It was simplicity itself: a chimney-like chamber, about 1m (3ft) square, in which four prisoners were placed. Ventilation of a sort was provided by a small opening in the ceiling. Crammed together, of necessity the prisoners were unable to do anything other than stand, hence the name. Sentences were generally for 72 hours of increasingly excruciating agony, during which the inmates might perhaps be fed a single loaf. Quite deliberately, the mental strain was at least as great as the physical deprivation.

The Nuremberg Laws of 1935 were exactly intended as a further tightening of the screw, stripping Jews of property rights, preventing them from holding government posts, forbidding marriages between Jews and non-Jews. Simultaneously, the pace of state-sanctioned, anti-Semitic violence was stepped up. Beatings, bombings and casual persecution became the norm. Jews were forbidden to use buses, to visit parks, to eat in almost all restaurants. Jewish businesses were likewise boycotted. To emigrate, Jews were effectively obliged to hand over up to 50 per cent of their assets to the government.

A grim racheting-up of this persecution occurred on the night of 9 November 1938. It was driven partly by the desire of its instigator, Joseph Goebbels, to re-ingratiate himself with Hitler, with whom he had fallen out of favour after taking up with a new mistress. Kristallnacht – the Night of Broken Glass – saw an apparently spontaneous series of anti-Jewish uprisings, in reality precisely co-ordinated over three days,

across the country. Over 30,000 Jews were arrested in its wake. It sparked a surge of frantic emigration among the country's remaining Jews. Hitler blamed it on Jewish agitation.

In 1933, the Jewish population of Germany was approximately 500,000. Between 1933 and 1939, an estimated 300,000 Jews left Germany, settling mostly in Britain, France, the United States and Palestine. Of the remaining 200,000-plus in 1939, scarcely 20,000 were alive in 1945.

BELOW Heinrich Himmler on a rare visit to Dachau near Munich, oldest of the Nazi's concentration camps. The SS chief was notoriously squeamish and hated the sight of blood.

OPPOSITE The front page of Der Stürmer *(The Attacker)* newspaper, *May 1934. Der Stürmer was a Nazi newspaper, founded in 1923 by Julius Streicher, himself executed at Nuremberg in 1946, given to crudely effective anti-Semitic propaganda. This edition from May 1934 shows Jews extracting blood from Christian children.*

Preis 30 Pfennig

Ritualmord-Nummer

Der Stürmer

Deutsches Wochenblatt zum Kampfe um die Wahrheit

HERAUSGEBER: JULIUS STREICHER

| Sonder-Nummer 7 | Erscheint wöchentl. Einz.-Nr. 30 Pfg. Bezugspreis monatl. 84 Pfg. zuzügl. Postbestellgeld. Bestellungen bei dem Briefträger oder der zuständ. Postanstalt. Nachdruck, a. d. Verlag. Schluß der Anzeigen- aufnahme: Montag vorm. 8 Uhr. Preis für Geschäfts-Anz.: Die ca. 21 mm breite, 1 mm hohe Raum-Zeile im Anzeigenteil —.15 RM. | Nürnberg, im Mai 1934 | Verlag: Hanns König, Nürnberg-O, Pfannenschmiedsgasse 19 Verlagsleitung: Max Fink, Nürnberg-O, Pfannenschmiedsgasse 19 Fernsprecher Nr. 21176. Postscheckkonto: Amt Nürnberg Nr. 105 Schriftleitung: Nürnberg-O, Marstallstr. 44, Fernsprecher 21176 Redaktionsschluß: Montag (nachmittags) | 12. Jahr 1934 |

Jüdischer Mordplan

gegen die nichtjüdische Menschheit aufgedeckt

Das Mördervolk

Die Juden stehen in der ganzen Welt in einem furcht- baren Verdacht. Wer ihn nicht kennt, der kennt die Ju- denfrage nicht. Wer die Juden nur ansieht, wie Heinrich Heine (Chaim Bückeburg) sie beschreibt: „Ein Volk, das zu seinem Unterhalt mit Wechseln und alten Hosen handelt und dessen Uniform die langen Nasen sind," der ist auf falschem Wege. Wer aber weiß, welch eine ungeheuerliche Anklage schon seit Anbeginn gegen die Juden erhoben wird, dem er- scheint dieses Volk in einem anderen Lichte. Er sieht in ihnen nicht nur ein eigenartiges, seltsam anmutendes Volk, er sieht in ihnen Verbrecher und Mörder und Teufel in Menschengestalt. Und es über- kommt ihn gegen dieses Volk ein heiliger Zorn und Haß.

Der Verdacht, in dem die Juden stehen, ist der des Menschenmordes. Sie werden bezichtigt, nicht- jüdische Kinder und nichtjüdische Erwachsene an sich zu locken, sie zu schlachten und ihnen das Blut abzuzapfen. Sie werden bezichtigt, dieses Blut in die Mazzen (un- gesäuertes Brot) zu verbacken und auch sonstige aber- gläubische Zauberei damit zu treiben. Sie werden be- zichtigt, ihre Opfer, besonders die Kinder, dabei furcht- bar zu martern und zu foltern. Und während dieses Folterns Drohungen, Flüche und Verwünschungen gegen die Nichtjuden auszustoßen. Dieser planmäßig betriebene Menschenmord hat eine besondere Bezeichnung, er heißt

Ritualmord.

Das Wissen vom jüdischen Ritualmord ist schon Jahr- tausende alt. Es ist so alt wie die Juden selbst. Die Nicht- juden haben es von Generation zu Generation übertragen. Es ist uns durch Schriften überliefert. Es ist aber auch in der breiten Volksmasse vorhanden. In den versteckten Bauerndörfern stößt man auf dieses Wissen. Der Ahne sprach von ihm zu seinem Enkel. Und dieser wieder trug es weiter auf Kinder und Kindeskinder. So vererbte es sich bis zum heutigen Tag.

Es ist auch in den anderen Völkern vorhanden. Wo irgendwo in der Welt eine Leiche gefunden wird, die die Anzeichen des Ritualmordes trägt, erhebt sich sofort laut und groß die Anklage. Sie richtet sich überall nur gegen die Juden. Hunderte und aberhunderte von Völkern, Stämmen und Rassen bewohnen den Erdball. Niemand denkt daran, sie des planmäßigen Kindermordes zu beschuldigen und sie als Mördervolk zu bezeichnen. Den Juden allein wird diese Anklage aus allen Völkern entgegengeschleudert. Und viele große Männer haben

Judenopfer

Durch die Jahrtausende vergoß der Jud, geheimem Ritus folgend, Menschenblut
Der Teufel sitzt uns heute noch im Nacken, es liegt an Euch die Teufelsbrut zu packen

Die Juden sind unser Unglück!

DIE POLIZEIVERWALTUNG ZERBST

Zahlungen nur auf
Konto Stadthauptkasse Zerbst bei der Kreissparkasse Zerbst

Postscheckkonto: Magdeburg 532 :: Fernruf: 8, 24, 41, 47, 63

An	Eingangs- und Bearbeitungsvermerke:
das Konzentrationslager	
O r a n i e n b u r g	

Ihr Zeichen:	Ihr Schreiben vom:	Unser Zeichen: P II 149/34	Datum:

Betrifft:

Anliegend übersenden wir hiermit einen photogra-
phischen Abzug einer schriftlichen Erklärung des ehemaligen
Schutzhäftlinges Wilhelm Jeremies über die Todesursache
des ehemaligen Schutzhäftlinges Max Sens zur weiteren Ver-
wendung.

Nach den von uns gemachten Feststellungen war Sens
bereits seit mehreren Jahren schwer herzkrank.

Zerbst, den 17. Februar 1934.

Die Polizeiverwaltung.

Notification of the death of a prisoner in the first concentration camp, 1934.

With reference to:
[illegible]

We hereby attach a photographic copy of a written declaration by the former protective custody prisoner Wilhelm Jeremies about the circumstances surrounding the death of former protective custody prisoner Max Sens for further use.

According to our findings, Sens had already suffered from a serious heart condition for several years.

Zerbst, 17 February 1934
The Police Administration

[Signature]

OPPOSITE In what would become only too frequent a development, a report from the Zerbst Police Administration in eastern Germany details the death in February 1934 of a prisoner, Max Sens, held in protective custody, reportedly from "a serious heart condition".

Wirtschafts- Verwaltungshauptamt   Oranienburg, den 11. Febr. 1943.
    Amtsgruppe D
  - Konzentrationslager -
D I/1 / Az.: 14 e 2 /Ot./ U.-
Geheim Tgb.-Nr. 111 / 43.

    Betreff: Häftlinge, die unter den "Keitel-Erlass"
              fallen.
    Bezug: Hies. Runderlass D I / Az.: 14 e 2 /Ot./ U.-
              Geheim Tgb.-Nr. 551 / 42 von 18.8.42.
    Anlagen: keine

                                        Geheim

    An die
    Lagerkommandanten der
    Konzentrationslager
    Da., Sch., Bu., Lau., Flo., Neu., Au., Gr.-Ro., Nats.,
    Nie., Stu., Bers., Rav. und Kriegsgef.-Lager Lublin.

    Vom Lagerkommandanten eines Konzentrationslagers wurde
    der Ehefrau eines verstorbenen französischen Häftlings,
    der in den Einweisungspapieren ausdrücklich als Häftling
    der Angelegenheit "Porto" gekennzeichnet war, der Toten-
    schein direkt übersandt, sodaß die Ehefrau vom Todesfall
    Kenntnis erhielt.

    Ich weise nochmals mit allem Nachdruck darauf hin, daß der
    mit dem oben angezogenen Geheim-Schreiben übersandte Aus-
    zug aus dem Nacht- und Nebel-Erlass strengstens zu beach-
    ten ist. Der Nacht- und Nebel-Erlass hat den Zweck, dritte
    Personen in den besetzten Gebieten über den Verbleib der
    ins Reich überführten Häftlinge im Unklaren zu lassen.
    Hierzu gehört auch, daß die Angehörigen nichts erfahren
    dürfen, wenn ein solcher Häftling in einem Konzentrations-
    lager stirbt.

    Der gesamte Schriftverkehr über Häftlinge, die unter den
    Nacht- und Nebel-Erlass fallen, hat nur mit den zuständigen

Dienststellen der Sipo unter "Geheim" zu erfolgen. Über den
Verbleib von Nacht- und Nebel-Häftlingen dürfen Zivilper-
sonen oder andere Dienststellen nichts erfahren.

Die Lagerkommandanten haben für Durchführung der vorstehenden Anordnung Sorge zu tragen.

                        Der Chef des Zentralamtes

                        // - Obersturmbannführer.

Night and Fog directives

Main Economic and Administrative Department Oranienburg, 11 February 1943.
Department D
– Concentration Camps – D I/1 / Az. :14 e 2 /Ot./ U.–
Secret Journal Entry No. 111 / 43

Subject: Prisoners who come under the Keitel Directive
Reference: Local [illegible] Circular Directive D I/1 / Az. :14 e 2 /
Ot./ U.–
Secret Journal Entry No. 551 / 42 dated 18.8.42.
Attachments: None

SECRET
To the
Camp Commandants of
Concentration camps
Da., Sah., Bu., Mau., Flo., Neu., Au., Gr.-Ro., Natz.,
Wie., Stu., Herz., Bav., and Lublin prisoner-of-war camp.

A concentration camp commandant sent the death certificate of a deceased French prisoner, who had expressly been identified as a "Porto" affair prisoner in the instruction papers, directly to his wife, who was made aware of his death as a result.

I reiterate in the strongest possible terms that the extract from the Night and Fog Directive cited above must be strictly observed. The aim of the Night and Fog Directive is to leave third parties in Occupied Territories in the dark as to the whereabouts of prisoners transferred to the Reich. To this end it is fitting that relatives must not find out if such a prisoner dies in a concentration camp.

All correspondence about prisoners who come under the Night and Fog Directive must take place only with the relevant SiPo departments and be marked "Secret". Civilians and other departments must not learn anything about the whereabouts of Night and Fog prisoners.

OPPOSITE AND FOLLOWING PAGES Two directives from the SS-WVHA, the SS Main Economic and Administrative Department, from February 1943 and February 1944, instructing camp commandants to implement the Nacht und Nebel *(Night and Fog) initiative, whereby political opponents of the Nazis were to disappear.*

irtschafts-Verwaltungshauptamt   Oranienburg,den 2.ebruar 1944.
tsgruppenchef D
- Konzentrationslager -

D I/Az.: 14 o 2/Ot/S.-
Geh.: Tgb.-Nr. 2o5/44

Betrifft: Verfolgung von Straftaten gegen das Reich oder die
      Besatzungsmacht in den besetzten Gebieten (Nacht-und
      Nebelerlaß).

Bezug: Reichssicherheitshauptamt -IV D 4- 1o3/43 g.-
      v.31.12.43.

Anlagen: -/-

An die
Lagerkommandanten der
Konzentrationslager

Da.,Sah.,Bu.,au.,Flo.,ou.,Au. I-III,Gr.-Ro.,Nats.,Stu.,Rav.,
Mors.,Lubl.,ar.,Gruppenleiter D u. ufemtl. Lager Berg.-Belo..

Nach Mitteilung des Reichssicherheitshauptamtes hat der Reichs-
minister der Justiz mit Erlaß an die Justizbehörden vom 6.3.1943
Tgb.-Nr. IV a - 398/43 g.- u.a. folgendes bestimmt:

" 7.Der Leichnam hingerichteter oder sonst verstorbener NN-
Gefangener wird der Stapoleizei zur Bestattung überwiesen.
Dabei ist auf die geltenden Geheimhaltungsvorschriften hinzu-
weisen. Mit Rücksicht auf diese ist insbesondere darauf hinzu-
wirken, daß die Gräber der NN-Gefangenen nicht durch Angabe
der Namen der Verstorbenen gekennzeichnet werden.
Von der Überlassung des Leichnams für Lehr- und Forschungs-
zwecke ist abzusehen".

Die von den Stapo-leit-stellen zur Inhaftierung in die Konz.-
lager gebrachten Leichen sind zu übernehmen und einzuäschern.
Hierzu wird folgendes angeordnet:

1.) Die vorstehenden Fälle müssen durch die Listen der Lager-
      Krematorien laufen.
2.) Die Asche ist in einer Urne aufzubewahren.
      Die Urnendeckel sind zu beschriften.
3.) Die Urnen sind bis auf weiteres in den Konzentrations-
      lagern aufzubewahren.

4.) Die Sterbeurkunden sind durch die lagereigenen Standes-
ämter auszustellen und dem Befehlshaber der Sicherheitspolizei und des SD in Paris mit dem Hinweis zu übersenden,
da es sich um verstorbene Nacht-und Nebelhäftlinge
handelt.

gez.

SS-Gruppenführer und
Generalleutnant der Waffen-SS

Main Economic and Administrative Department   Oranienburg, February 1944.
Head of Department D
– Concentration Camps –
D I/1 / Az. :14 c 2 /Ot./ S.–
Secret Journal Entry No. 205 / 44

Subject: Prosecution of crimes against the Reich or the Occupying
Forces in the Occupied Territories (Night and Fog Directive).
Reference: Reich Security Head Office –IV B 4- 1o3/4 g. – of 31.12.43
Attachments:-/-

[stamp] SECRET

To the
Camp Commandants of
Concentration camps
Da., Sah., Bu., Mau., Flo., Neu., Au.I-III, Gr.-Ro., Natz.,Stu., Rav.,
Herz., Lubl., .ar., Group leader D and Holding Camp Berg.-Bels..

Following notification by the Reich Security Head Office, the Reich Minister of Justice has
ordered the following, inter alia, in the Directive to the Judicial Authorities, Journal No. IV a –
398/43 g. dated 6.3.1943:

"7. The body of executed or otherwise deceased prisoners must be handed over to the State
Police for burial. Attention is thereby drawn to the applicable regulations for maintaining
secrecy. Taking these into account, special care should be taken not to identify the graves of NN
prisoners by name. Giving the body over for teaching or research purposes must be avoided."

The bodies brought into the concentration camps by the State Police headquarters for the
purposes of cremation must be accepted and incinerated.
To this end, the following instructions apply:
1.) The abovementioned cases must be processed through the lists of the camp crematoria.
2.) The ashes must be stored in an urn.
    The urn lid should be marked.
3.) The urns should be kept in the concentration camps until further notice.
4) Notifications of death must be registered with the camps' internal records office and notified
to the commander of the Security Police and Security Service in Paris, indicating that the case
involves a deceased Night and Fog prisoner.

[signature, illegible]

SS-Gruppenführer and
Generalleutnant of the Waffen-SS

Poland Invaded

That Hitler expected a European war is plain, even if he assumed it would not come until perhaps 1942. From 1936, a clear pattern of aggressive expansion developed: the remilitarization of the Rhineland; the absorption of Austria *(Anschluss)* in March 1938; the take-over of western Czechoslovakia the following autumn and the absorption of the rest of the country the following March. The stage was set.

This expansion highlighted a consistent feature: that Hitler was a masterful bluffer. He had faced down Britain and France in Munich in 1938 when they attempted to prevent the Nazi absorption of the Sudetenland in Czechoslovakia by promising that he had no further territorial ambitions in Czechoslovakia. In exactly the same way, though rearmament had greatly increased Germany's military capacity, he repeatedly exaggerated Germany's real military strength. In August 1939, he produced perhaps his most audacious stroke: an alliance with the Soviet Union that nullified the threat from the Soviet Union by allowing the Soviets a free hand in eastern Poland while Germany took over the west of the country. In effect, Poland was partitioned.

On 1 September, Germany duly invaded Poland, prompting declarations of war against Germany by Poland's allies, Britain and France on 3 September, not that there was anything either country could do to defend the Poles. The Soviet invasion followed on 17 September. With the bulk of the Polish army in the west of the country, the Soviets advanced largely unopposed. By 28 September, Warsaw had capitulated to the Nazis.

The most notable feature of the Polish campaign was not how swift it was. The disparity in forces – 55 German divisions, a number heavily mechanized, against 39 Polish divisions and 11 cavalry brigades; 1,929 German aircraft against 200 Polish – made German victory assured. Rather it was the treatment of the Poles themselves. To prevent the possibility of future Polish resistance, the structure of Polish society was to be destroyed. Hitler was explicit on the point: "There must be no Polish leaders; where Polish leaders exist they must be killed, however harsh that sounds". Teachers, politicians, intellectuals, the clergy, industrialists, anyone around whom the kernel of a future Polish state could form, were all to be murdered. Lists of those to be killed had been drawn up by the SS over the summer.

To achieve this, seven *Einsatzgruppen*, or Deployment Groups, in reality mobile killing units, consisting of police and members of the SS under the control of Reinhard Heydrich and first used in Austria in 1938, were sent to Poland. They totalled about 2,700 men. Though they operated alongside regular army units, they were independent of them. They were supported by units of paramilitary *Volksdeutscher Selbstschutz,* or Self-Defence Activists, ethnic Germans in Poland who were trained in sabotage and guerrilla tactics by the Germans.

Their targets were almost exclusively civilians. By the end of the year, their victims numbered around 65,000, all peremptorily shot in executions large and small. It was behaviour that appalled many German soldiers. Those who complained, such as General Johannes Blaskowitz, who commanded the German 8th Army in the invasion, were scorned by Hitler for their "misplaced humanitarianism", which in Blaskowitz's case saw him relieved of his command the following May.

In much the same way, the Poles were then to be "mentally enfeebled", turned into a drudge slave race. Meanwhile, their primary task accomplished, the *Einsatzgruppen* were directed to turn their attentions to a new task: the herding of Poland's Jews into ghettos.

Operation Himmler

Even by the Nazis' gangster standards, their justification for the invasion of Poland in 1939 was extraordinarily cynical. The Germans claimed to be doing no more than responding to acts of Polish provocation: raids by Polish troops on German border posts and the harassment and execution of ethnic Germans in Poland. The reality was that, under Operation Himmler, any such apparently unprovoked raids were carried out by SS troops in Polish uniforms. Dead Polish soldiers supposedly killed by the Germans in self-defence were Polish political prisoners who had been murdered by the Nazis before being dressed as Polish troops.

OPPOSITE Goose-stepping into history: German troops march through Warsaw after the capitulation of the Polish capital.

BELOW It is a central tenet of Orthodox Judaism that men should not shave. Following their invasion of Poland, Nazi troops took particular pleasure in humiliating Jews by crudely hacking off their beards.

Ghettos: Deliberate Deprivation

Following their conquest of western Poland, home to more than two million Jews, the Nazi response was partly to force as many Jews as possible into Soviet-controlled eastern Poland. More particularly, it was to drive those that remained, the vast majority, into a series of ghettos, in effect prisons, across the country. If never more than a short-term solution, the result was suffering on an epic scale.

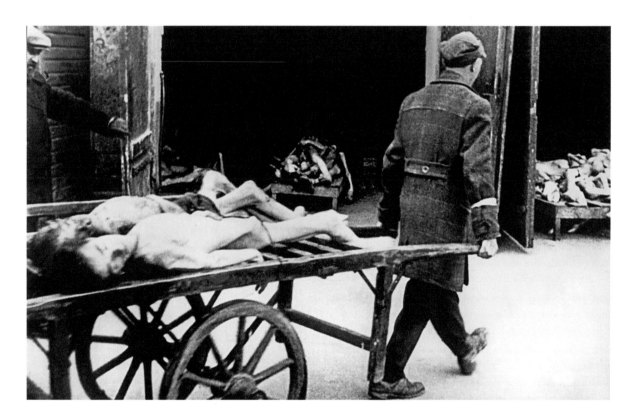

From the establishment of the first ghetto in Poland, Piotrków Tryunalski, in October 1939 to the destruction of the last, Lódz (Litzmannstadt), in August 1944, in excess of 1,000 Jewish ghettos were created by the Nazis. Most contained only a few thousand, some just a few hundred; many were little more than transit camps. By contrast, the largest, in Warsaw, Lódz and Lwów, contained respectively 450,000, 200,000 and 150,000 Jews. All three were in the General Government, the area of central Poland not absorbed into the German Reich but effectively re-cast as a German colony. To all intents and purposes, it was a 20th-century slave state.

However short-lived, the major ghettos in particular, blandly known by the Nazis as *Jüdischer Wohnbezirk* or Jewish Quarters, were unique worlds: oppressed, impoverished, deprived. Their most immediately obvious feature was overcrowding. Warsaw in 1939 was the second-largest Jewish city in the world, behind only New York, its Jewish inhabitants accounting for almost one-third of the entire population of the city. Yet the city's Jews, their numbers boosted by an influx of Jewish refugees fleeing the initial German advance as well as those subsequently forcibly resettled by the Germans, were then crammed into an area of 1.3 square miles, less than 3 per cent of Warsaw's total extent.

An extraordinary underworld developed, of illicit dealings, of smuggling, of perilous contacts with what was known as the "Aryan Side". It was driven by fear, hunger, disease and impoverishment. The Jews were forbidden on pain of instant execution to leave the ghetto, now surrounded by a crudely built, barbed-wire-topped brick wall, permanently guarded. Faced with the starvation rations provided by the Germans of 184 calories per person per day (the average adult requires around 2,500), children in particular were routinely sent across the wall to scavenge for what food they could. At the same time, the Germans demanded punitive financial payments, in effect insisting the Jews meet the cost of their incarceration. The result was savings rapidly exhausted, followed by almost no prospect of any kind of legal employment to meet the cost of even the most basic daily needs.

An inevitable consequence was the spread of disease; typhus and cholera above all. Emaciated corpses slumped in doorways, or collapsed on pavements, became a routine sight. It was in part the realization that these diseases would spread beyond the ghettos, in part the impossibility of squeezing even more Jews into such already squalidly over-crowded quarters, that prompted the Nazi rulers of the General Government to argue for the extermination of the Jews. In the meantime, bitter winter temperatures brought an inevitable extra cost in deaths, the old and the young suffering disproportionately.

It was a final, bitter twist of Nazi rule that the Jews were obliged to administer themselves on behalf of their German overlords through a series of *Judenraete* or Jewish Councils. It was the *Judenraete*, for example, who were forced to provide the names of Jews who, from July 1942, were to be sent to the East for "resettlement", meaning extermination. On 22 July 1942, Adam Czerniakow, head of the Warsaw *Judenrat*, killed himself when his pleas that orphans in the Warsaw ghetto not be resettled were refused. He had been brought face to face with a simple truth: Poland's Jews could expect no hope of any accommodation with Nazi rule.

OPPOSITE The dead of the Warsaw Ghetto literally carted away, 1943. Early every morning, those who had died on the streets would be collected for cremation.

BELOW The blank, hastily built wall of the Warsaw Ghetto, enclosing a world of acute and enduring suffering.

Jewish Ghetto police

In much the same way that the Nazis obliged the *Judenraete* to oversee the day-to-day administration of the ghettos, so they forced them to establish the *Jüdische Ordnungsdienst*, the Jewish Ghetto Police, to impose order. These were Jews, rarely from the areas they policed, whose duties were to act as surrogate Nazis in imposing Nazi rule. They tended, perhaps inevitably, to be unusually thuggish, revelling in their new authority, for all that they had no official uniforms and, like all ghetto Jews, were obliged to wear a Star of David on their right arms. Their reward, as the ghettos were destroyed, was to be sent to the death camps in their turn.

BELOW Jewish Ghetto Police in Warsaw, 1941. They may have been an ad hoc force but they lacked for nothing in brutality.

RIGHT A painting by Halina Olomucki from the Warsaw Ghetto. Halina Olomucki, born in Warsaw in 1919, incarcerated in the Warsaw ghetto and sent in 1943 to Auschwitz, was one of a handful of Jews who produced a visual record of their experiences. Women and children – here a family in the ghetto – were her principal subjects.

Operation Barbarossa

Hitler never made any secret that his eventual goal was the destruction of the Soviet Union. This was where the final, elemental struggle between the Nazis and what he cast as the Jewish Bolshevik conspiracy would take place. It was, Hitler believed, a conflict that would decisively shape humanity's future. The consequence was a war of unprecedented savagery, of two bitterly opposed totalitarian ideologies fighting to the death.

When the Nazi Invasion of the Soviet Union was launched on 22 June 1941 – Operation Barbarossa – the two states were still nominally allies. Stalin, leader of the Soviet Union, a man whose brutal treatment of his enemies arguably exceeded even Hitler's, was left dazed. For nearly two weeks, he disappeared.

By the time he had reasserted his leadership, the Soviet cause looked doomed. In what seemed a precise echo of their campaigns against the West the previous year, Axis forces, three million strong, swept into the Soviet Union along a front of almost 1,600 km (approximately 1,000 miles). Numerically stronger or not, the Soviet armies were powerless to resist them.

A series of massive pincer movements, headed by Panzer and other motorized divisions, encircled entire Soviet armies. Over two million Soviet men were captured. In their wake followed the *Einsatzgruppen*, unleashing a wave of mass slaughter (*see* pages 40–41). By the early autumn, the initial Soviet numerical superiority in tanks and planes had been wiped out, Leningrad was surrounded and Moscow threatened.

Hitler gloated in what now seemed absolute victory, boasting that the whole of the western Soviet Union was to be incorporated within the Third Reich, settled by Germans who would exploit its immense agricultural resources while the residue of its impoverished Slav peoples was banished far to the east beyond the Urals. A New Order, dominated by Germany, would be created.

Whatever these early successes, the Nazi advance was less assured than it appeared, critically depending on speed and surprise. Nazi Germany may have invaded the Soviet Union with 3,350 tanks and the same number of planes, but it also did so with 650,000 horses. And it was the horses that dictated the ultimate pace of the invasion. For all Hitler's boasting, his armies were unable to advance faster than Napoleon's over a century earlier.

Any delay was potentially disastrous, exposing the Germans, so confident of victory that supply lines were neglected and winter clothing not issued, to the brutal reality of a Russian winter. The Nazis similarly failed to take into the account the Soviet capacity for improvisation: in training and mobilizing huge new armies; in relocating entire factories – over 1,500 – away from the fighting, where they then produced huge numbers of weapons.

In December 1941, the German advance stalled on the outskirts of Moscow. When it was renewed the following spring, impressive early gains, above all towards the oil-rich Caucasus, proved equally illusory, ultimately falling victim not just to geography and a further Russian winter, but also to the exceptional fighting spirit of the Soviet forces. Though obliged to endure conditions infinitely harder than any experienced in the West and to suffer enormous casualties, at least 10.6 million, the Red Army would eventually prove crushingly superior. The surrender of the German 6th Army at Stalingrad on 2 February 1943, having suffered 400,000 casualties, proved decisive.

Hitler's great 20th-century crusade to rid the world of the plague of "Judeo-Bolshevism and the Slavic menace" would in the end only ensure the final defeat of Nazism.

ABOVE November 1941 near Moscow: Hitler's expectations of swiftly smashing the Soviets came face to face with the Russian winter and overstretched supply lines. The horses suffered as much as the men. It was the first serious check the Nazis faced.

OPPOSITE Soviet troops marched to captivity and probable death pass fresh German troops moving up the front in early July 1941.

The Siege of Leningrad

However appalling the siege of Stalingrad, it at least had the virtue of being comparatively short lived – five months. That of Leningrad lasted almost two-and-a-half years, from 8 September 1941 to 27 January 1944. It produced an epic of suffering. In the region of 900,000 died out of a pre-war population of 2.5 million, the majority from starvation. By December 1941, a month in which 52,000 died, its inhabitants were subsisting on flour made from shell packing and bread from wallpaper paste. What horses, dogs and cats there had once been had all been eaten. The city's sewers were also destroyed by shelling and the stock of medicines ran out.

RIGHT Victims of the siege awaiting burial at the city's Volkovo cemetery. The death toll mounted remorselessly.

Slaughter Unleashed:

Einsatzgruppen

Exactly as in Poland, the German forces that invaded the Soviet Union were accompanied by *Einsatzgruppen*. There were no more than four, designated A, B, C and D. Their total numbers were scarcely 3,000. Yet they unleashed a wave of indiscriminate and relentless killing. Their notional targets were communists, Jews, agitators and other "enemies of the state". In reality, the Jews were their particular target. By late August 1941, the killings began in earnest.

Shortly before Operation Barbarossa was launched in the early summer of 1941, Hitler had exempted all German troops from the provisions of the Hague Conventions governing the treatment of civilians and prisoners. For Hitler, whose contempt for notions of ordinary morality was absolute, this was no more than logical: in such a desperate clash of civilizations, every means should be mobilized to secure victory. At much the same time, in his Commissar Order of March 1941 he decreed that "unhesitatingly severe measures" (a characteristic Nazi euphemism for murder) be taken against all communist officials.

After the invasion began, Reinhard Heydrich progressively widened the scope of the Order. On 2 July, he declared that "other radical elements" were to be eliminated; then that all Jewish men between the ages of 15 and 45 be eliminated and in August that all Jews, henceforth designated as "partisans", be eliminated. This was perhaps the single most decisive step towards the Final Solution.

At the same time, the *Einsatzgruppen* encouraged the activities of local anti-Semitic groups. This proved particularly effective in Baltic States, tapping not just a deep-rooted anti-Semitism but also a belief that Jews had conspired to bring about the annexation of the Baltic States by Stalin the year before. By the end of 1941, the most notorious of these, the Arajs Kommando, had wiped out almost half of Latvia's pre-invasion Jewish population of 83,000. By December, only 3,500 Latvian Jews remained; by the end of the war, 800. Local police forces were similarly effective in rounding up Jews. Many also participated in the executions.

The killings were far from the exclusive preserve of the *Einsatzgruppen* and local groupings. The army itself was active in perpetrating atrocities as well as lending logistical and other support to the *Einsatzgruppen*. In October 1941, Field Marshal von Reichenau issued what was known as the Severity Order, which called for the "just retribution that must be meted out to the sub-human species of Jewry".

While there were a number of major massacres, most obviously at Rumbula in Latvia and Babi Yar in the Ukraine (*see* pages 42–43), the majority of the killing was on a smaller scale. Typically, the victims would be required to assemble for "resettlement". They were then forced to hand over valuables and money before being ordered to undress. Next, they would be herded into pits, often dug by Soviet prisoners, then shot. On 29 October 1941 at Kaunas in Lithuania, for example, *Einsatzgruppe* A oversaw the execution of 2,007 men, 2,920 women and 4,273 children. It was a routine operation.

Not the least remarkable feature of at least some of the killing is that it was meticulously recorded. The Jäger Report, so-called as it was compiled by an SS colonel, Karl Jäger, details with extraordinary precision the deaths of 137,346 Lithuanians between 2 July and 25 November 1941. All but 1,851 were Jews.

That said, the total number of victims of the *Einsatzgruppen* and their collaborators can never be known. The most commonly accepted figure is two million.

OPPOSITE RIGHT Field Marshal Walter von Reichenau, author of the Severity Order. He died, of a heart attack, only three months later.

OPPOSITE LEFT German troops pose in front of a burnt synagogue in Bialystok in northeast Poland, an image captured in 1941.

BELOW LEFT Humiliation, degradation, death: Jewish women forced to strip before their inevitable execution.

ABOVE Vinnitsa, the Ukraine, 1942: a partially filled mass grave, a kneeling Jew, his executioner. In the background, Einsatzgruppen *troops look on with stoic indifference.*

The Trauma of Terror

It was an enduring irony of the *Einsatzgruppen* that, however many they killed, it was never enough. Put crudely, shooting their victims was too slow and uncertain a way of eradicating the Soviet Union's millions of racial inferiors. A faster, more certain guarantee of death was needed. At the same time, even the most hardened of the *Einsatzgruppen* became progressively demoralized with their endless execution of the obviously innocent. A morose, alcohol-fuelled torpor spread through their ranks. Himmler, in particular, was concerned at this lowering of morale. It prompted his support for a new, more reliable means of mass execution: gas chambers.

Babi Yar: Anatomy of a Massacre

Babi Yar, a ravine just outside Kiev, capital of the Ukraine, was the site of the largest single mass execution of the Second World War. On 29 and 30 September 1941, units of *Einsatzgruppe C*, aided by Ukranian police, shot 33,771 Jews. The site thereafter was consistently used by the Germans for executions, not just of further Jews but of gypsies and other "undesirables". An estimated 80,000-plus met their deaths here.

The attraction of Babi Yar as a place of murder to the Germans was partly its closeness to Kiev, more particularly because it was a ravine, 152.5m (500ft) long, 21.3m (70ft) wide, and 15.25m (50ft) deep. In other words, it spared the Germans the necessity of digging pits in which to bury the dead. The victims could simply be shot, either on the rim or on the floor of the ravine itself. Either way, they would then be covered with earth. Further victims could be processed in the same way, the corpses accumulating layer by layer.

The September killings were both part of the *Einsatzgruppe*'s mission as a whole, more specifically retaliation for a number of bombs in Kiev, which had fallen to the Germans on 19 September, in which several hundred German soldiers were killed. The bombs were the work of underground Soviet NKVD agents. The Germans presumed they were the work of Jews.

On 28 September, notices were posted instructing the city's Jews to assemble, on pain of death, at a designated site in the city at 8.00 the following morning. By this point, the Jewish population of Kiev (160,000 in 1939) had been substantially reduced by those fleeing east to escape the Germans. That said, there were still an estimated 60,000.

ABOVE Naked bodies at Babi Yar, slaughtered indiscriminately, hurled into a mass grave, innocent victims of Nazi bestiality.

OPPOSITE RIGHT Further slaughter at Babi Yar. Chillingly, this picture was later found among the personal effects of a dead German officer, who evidently had little compunction in carrying around so disturbing an image.

The Germans expected perhaps 5,000 or 6,000 to show up. The actual number was over 30,000, taken in by the promise of "resettlement". Why else would they have been expected to bring winter clothing and valuables? As they were herded towards Babi Yar, the belief spread that it was a railway junction they were making for. There, surely, the trains to take them to the east would be waiting. Salvation, of a kind, was always easier to believe in than imminent execution.

What unfolded would become numbingly familiar. After inevitable delays, the Jews were shuffled slowly forward. Reaching a Jewish cemetery, which in a less than subtle irony was next to the ravine, they were ordered to leave their suitcases and valuables (all of which were later carefully sorted through by the Germans: "millions" of bank notes were reported as having been found). Continuing forwards, they were made to strip, their clothes placed in precise piles. Then, in groups of ten, they were funnelled between lines of troops. Any who hesitated were beaten with clubs and rifle butts.

By now, as the sound of shots rang out, those nearing the ravine were not just being forced onward by the soldiers on either side but also pressed forward by the crowds behind, who in many cases were still unaware of the killings. Reaching the ravine, they were peremptorily shot.

In the confusion, unknowable numbers were not killed cleanly. Their fate was to be buried alive. Later, hoping to speed the killings, the Germans would press two or more of their victims' heads together so as to kill both with one bullet.

Those whom the Germans had been unable to shoot immediately were held overnight in a series of compounds before they were executed the following day.

Dina Pronicheva (1911–77)

It is surprising that there were any survivors at all at Babi Yar. In fact, 28 are known to have lived, of which the best known was a Jewish actress, Dina Pronicheva. After the war, she recounted how she flung herself into the ravine before being shot, miming death, "the whole mass of bodies moving slightly as they settled down". A soldier trod on her at one point, then deliberately kicked her apparently lifeless form. As earth was shovelled on the bodies, she decided she would prefer to be shot than buried alive, scrambling her way to the surface and, in the dark, to improbable freedom.

LEFT Dina Pronicheva (foreground), photographed at a war trials investigation in Kiev in 1946. She died in 1977.

The Hunger Plan

The German goal in the invasion of the Soviet Union was more than just the conquest of territory. It was to rid those territories of their inhabitants. Himmler believed 30–50 million would need to die. Mass slaughter was one means of achieving this. Death camps would subsequently become another. But the Nazis simultaneously adopted a tactic that held even greater promise. The peoples of the conquered territories would be starved to death.

ABOVE Herbert Backe: the Nazi apparatchik personified – precise, bespectacled, ever deliberate.

LEFT Soviet refugees thronging roads under armed escort were an inevitable accompaniment to the endorsed starvation of millions.

OPPOSITE ABOVE Degradation, disease, despair, death: the reality of Nazi conquest.

The advantages were as obvious as the means were simple. All foodstuffs produced in the invaded lands would be seized to feed Germans, averting the near famine conditions the country had undergone at the end of the First World War. It would necessarily follow that those deprived – whether communists, Slavs, Jews or gypsies – would die in the resulting famine or be forced into exile. Either way, at no cost, Germany would have guaranteed its own food supplies while ensuring the extermination of millions of its enemies.

This was a deliberate aim, a core element of the plan, drawn up from early 1941, to invade the Soviet Union just as it was a core element in the later, planned, huge-scale German colonization of the lands of the western Soviet Union. Expressed in a series of droningly dead-pan memos and reports, it bore all the hallmarks of the Nazi bureaucratic mind at its most self-satisfied and callous.

Though the work of a series of different government departments, overall responsibility for the Hunger Plan, or *Hungerplan*, fell on the Reich Minister of Food, a comparatively junior official, Herbert Backe, a member of the Nazi Party since 1925, of the SS since 1933. It was enthusiastically endorsed by the Nazi leadership and, importantly, by the

army, who understood precisely its implications for the Soviet Union's ability to continue the war against Germany.

If the eventual German defeat meant that the longer-term goals of the plan would never be implemented, its short-term effects were devastating enough. No less than the Final Solution proper, they amounted to a precisely planned genocide, though Backe generously allowed that perhaps 14 million Slavs might later be kept alive as slave labourers.

It had two basic elements. The first was the confiscation of agricultural land, its farmers driven off. This would have an immediate impact on the Soviet Union's urban populations, by far the largest proportion of the overall Soviet population, who at a stroke would be cut off from food supplies. By extension, it would simultaneously cripple Soviet industry, assiduously and largely successfully expanded under Stalin in a series of Five-Year Plans, in the process emasculating Soviet armaments production.

The second was that it made the treatment of Soviet POWs exceptionally easy to implement. Once herded into a series of vast camps, they could then be abandoned as what the Germans called "superfluous mouths" to their inevitable, lingering fate (*see* pages 46–47).

In much the same way, even if not formally a part of the Hunger Plan, the Jews of the ghettos, both in Poland and the Soviet Union, could also slowly be left to die. In the end, this was a decision more or less reversed when it was decided that their deaths could more readily be assured in death camps.

From 1943, the Hunger Plan was similarly modified to the extent that, with Germany now at risk of defeat in the East, the value of Slavs and POWs as slave labour was too important to be ignored. But by then, close on 4.2 million had already died as a direct consequence of Backe's technocratic ingenuity.

Famine in the Ukraine

Exactly as eastern Poland – obliged to endure the triple trauma of an initial Soviet take-over in 1939, German invasion in 1941 and Soviet re-conquest in 1944 – reeled from catastrophe to catastrophe throughout the war, so the Hunger Plan dealt a peculiarly shocking blow to the inhabitants of the Ukraine. In 1932–3, 7.5 million Ukranians had died in a famine, the Holodomor or Terror Famine, brought about by Stalin's determination to collectivize agricultural production by bringing it under state control. Ten years later, the Ukraine endured a similarly appalling fate, the difference this time only that now the Nazis were the agents of terror.

RIGHT Ukrainians pack eggs for German troops. A propaganda picture taken to demonstrate the humane treatment of the Ukrainians. The reality was starkly different.

Soviet POWs: a Mere Statistic

Six months after Nazi Germany invaded the Soviet Union on 22 June 1941, 3.2 million Soviet troops had been captured by the Nazis. By the spring of 1942, about 2.8 million of them were dead, starved by their captors. By the end of the war, of the estimated 5.7 million Soviet troops captured by the Germans, approximately 3.3 million died. It was a death rate unmatched in any other theatre of the war.

The initial success of the Nazi invasion of eastern Poland and the Soviet Union in June 1941 was not due to any numerical advantage on the part of the Germans. Rather, it was a reflection of a series of Soviet miscalculations. First, that Stalin seemed unable to believe that his erstwhile ally would launch an invasion, despite mounting evidence to the contrary. Second, as a direct consequence, that the Soviet forces were unprepared to resist any major offensive, with most Soviet troops stationed far to the east. Third, whatever its size, the Soviet forces were in the midst of a major reorganization brought about by Stalin's brutal purging of almost all its senior officers between 1937 and 1939, and were accordingly crippled by a lack of intelligent leadership. An immense army, over five million strong, practically offered itself as a sacrificial victim.

As mounting numbers of Soviet forces fell into German hands, their fate became increasingly clear. Lacking the means to sustain a long-term conflict, Hitler had gambled everything on a swift victory. If it were taken as read that huge numbers of Soviets would be captured, no German plan existed for their treatment beyond the fact that, once captured, they could be directed into vast, hastily contrived camps, generally no more than immense open areas with no buildings and surrounded by barbed-wire. There, they could be abandoned. Their subsequent slow deaths from starvation and disease were taken not just as a given but also as a positive additional step in depopulating the Soviet Union. As their numbers shrank, those who remained, their clothes

frequently expropriated by the Germans, were forced to seek shelter in holes burrowed into the ground. In desperation, they ate leaves and grass. Cannibalism was rife.

In the longer term, Soviet re-armament and reorganization would eventually halt and then push back the Nazi advance. In the shorter term, suffering on a scale that remains numbing duly followed. This was the Holocaust recast; a casual extermination of vast numbers left with no means either to feed or clothe themselves. First in their hundreds, then their thousands, then their hundreds of thousands, they were purposefully left to die. Of all Soviet POWs in German captivity, an estimated 57 per cent died.

(By comparison, 3.6 per cent of all British POWs held by the Germans died in captivity.) The death rate of those who died in the first six months after Operation Barbarossa exceeded even that of the death camps at their peak.

OPPOSITE Near Kharkov in Ukraine: yet another endless, shuffling mass of Soviet prisoners being herded to their hideous fate.

ABOVE Soviet troops, harassed and haggard, following the German capture of the Kerch Peninsula in the Crimea.

They didn't merely die in the camps: as many as 400,000 Soviet POWs are believed to have died on a 150-mile forced march between the cities of Gzhatsk and Smolensk. Countless others were simply shot out of hand.

From 1942, as the need to put the German economy on a much more efficient war footing became urgent, the Germans increasingly sought to exploit their Soviet prisoners as slave labour. In effect, it meant little more than a different way of dying. Fifteen thousand Soviets were used in the expansion of Auschwitz, for example. Fewer than 100 survived.

ABOVE Soviet prisoners, shaved and naked before being disinfected, at one of the most notorious and largest slave labour camps, Mauthausen-Gusen near Linz in Austria.

OPPOSITE A letter from Hermann Göring, dated 31 July 1941, to Reinhard Heydrich instructing him to implement promptly the "organizational, practical and material measures" of the Final Solution – the endlösung *– of "the Jewish question" – der Judenfrage vorzulegen.*

Order 270

On August 16 1941, Stalin issued Order 270. In it, he asserted that any Soviet soldiers who surrendered to the Germans, whatever the circumstances, would be regarded as having betrayed the Motherland. "There are no Soviet prisoners of War," he declared, "only traitors." Instead, they were ordered to fight either until they were killed or killed themselves. His attitude to Soviet POWs who survived the war was equally uncompromising. Of an estimated 1.5 million POWs repatriated to the Soviet Union after the war, many by force, almost 250,000 were subsequently sent to the Gulag. Countless others were simply executed.

A letter from Hermann Göring to Reinhard Heydrich regarding the Final Solution

The Reichsmarschall of the Greater German   Berlin, July 1941
Reich   [initials]

Plenipotentiary of the Four Year Plan

President
of the Cabinet Council for the Defence of the Reich

         [initials]

To the
     Chief of the Security Police and Security Service   [164]
     SS-Gruppenführer Heydrich
     <u>Berlin.</u>

In addition to the task assigned to you by the Directive of 24.1.39, to provide the most favourable solution under the time circumstances to the Jewish question in the form of emigration or evacuation, I hereby instruct you to make all the necessary preparations from an organizational, practical and material point of view for a complete solution to the Jewish question within the German sphere of influence in Europe.

If the responsibilities of other central authorities are affected by this, they must be involved.

I further instruct you to submit to me in the near future an overall plan relating to the organizational, practical and material preparatory measures required for the implementation of the desired final solution of the Jewish question.

         [signature]

Murder Sanctioned:
the Wannsee Conference

For the Nazis, the Jews may always have been a subspecies, but Nazi treatment of the Jews changed significantly as the war continued, not least as Germany found itself absorbing huge new Jewish populations through conquest; two million in Poland alone. Yet it was only in 1941, after the invasion of the Soviet Union, itself home to 2.5 million Jews, that a Final Solution was decided on: the extermination of the Jews in their entirety.

An entire continent?

It was a measure either of the unreality of the Wannsee Conference – the fate of millions decided in a haze of cigar smoke and cognac fumes – or of its unwavering pragmatism that it anticipated not just the extinction of Jews in territories controlled by Nazi Germany but also the extinction of Jews in territories Germany neither controlled nor could realistically expect to control. It called for the eventual murder of all Britain's and Ireland's Jews, for example, respectively an additional 330,000 and 4,000 Jews. In rendering the whole of Europe *Judenfrei*, "free of Jews", it assumed a final death toll of 11 million.

In 1940, the Germans proposed, quite seriously, that Europe's Jews be forcibly resettled on the Indian Ocean island of Madagascar. For the scheme to work, however, Britain had first to be defeated so that its merchant fleet could be commandeered to transport the Jews. It was similarly critical that there be no resistance from the Royal Navy.

By the autumn of 1940, with Britain obstinately undefeated, enforced expulsion of Jews still remained the preferred Nazi option. Again, however, this was dependent on military success, this time against the Soviet Union, the distant wastes of Siberia now the preferred dumping ground for Europe's Jews.

As the Nazi assault against the Soviet Union stalled on the outskirts of Moscow in December 1941, it became evident that the war was set to drag on into at least a further year. Even if only temporarily, the Siberian option would have to be postponed.

The perverted logic of Nazi anti-Semitism also maintained that the recent entrance of the United States into the war after the bombing of Pearl Harbor by Germany's Japanese allies on 7 December 1941 was the direct consequence of malign manipulating by the country's Jewish puppet-masters, set on their sinister desire to dominate the world. Given the known efficacy of gas as means of murder, already being used to eradicate the physically and mentally handicapped (*see* pages 68–69), could this not be employed as a new, more certain answer to the Jewish question?

Clearly, these were significant and pressing reasons why Nazi Germany now decided that a Final Solution, the mass murder of the Jews, be adopted. But overwhelmingly the most important factor was Hitler himself. Increasingly convinced of his greatness, wholly in thrall to his love of violence, above all perhaps unable to see the world as anything other than an unrelenting struggle for supremacy between races, a kind of hideous Darwinism writ large, with himself its ultimate arbiter, it was his decision in the autumn of 1941 that Germany commit itself to the eradication of Europe's Jews. It was – and is – unthinkable that so radical a step in a country so entirely dominated by him could have been taken without his express

OPPOSITE 56–58 Am Grossen, Wannsee, bought by the SS late in 1940 on the recommendation of Heydrich, who was particularly struck by the excellent possibilities it offered for bathing and boating, as a guest house for senior SS personnel. Today it is a museum charting the history of the Holocaust.

ABOVE SS-Obergruppenführer Reinhard Heydrich in 1940. Three months after the conference, he was killed in Prague by Czech partisans. In revenge, the Germans killed at least 1,300 Czechs.

approval. Tellingly, Hitler's orders were never formalized on paper: they remained verbal. But then, as Führer, his will rarely needed to be formally expressed: instant obedience was taken as read. To the end, Hitler, while revelling in the destruction he had wrought, remained determined to shield the Germans from the barbarities he enacted on their behalf.

On 20 January 1942, in an opulent, early 20th-century, lakeside villa owned by the SS in Wannsee in the leafy suburbs of Berlin, a conference, chaired by SS General Reinhard Heydrich, acting on the express orders of Himmler, was held. As well as Heydrich, 14 other men attended, all high-ranking officials, civilian and military. In no more than an hour and a half the practical means of implementing this Final Solution were agreed. There was no debate as to the desirability of the goal, none of its morality. The intention, simply, was to agree the most effective means of putting it into practice.

ABOVE The lavishly appointed conference room where the fate of millions was decided.

The Wannsee Protocol

30 Ausfertigungen
16. Ausfertigung

Besprechungsprotokoll.

I. An der am 20.1.1942 in Berlin, Am Großen Wannsee Nr. 56/58, stattgefundenen Besprechung über die Endlösung der Judenfrage nahmen teil:

Gauleiter Dr. Meyer und Reichsamtsleiter Dr. Leibbrandt — Reichsministerium für die besetzten Ostgebiete

Staatssekretär Dr. Stuckart — Reichsministerium des Innern

Staatssekretär Neumann — Beauftragter für den Vierjahresplan

Staatssekretär Dr. Freisler — Reichsjustizministerium

Staatssekretär Dr. Bühler — Amt des Generalgouverneurs

Unterstaatssekretär Luther — Auswärtiges Amt

SS-Oberführer Klopfer — Partei-Kanzlei

Ministerialdirektor Kritzinger — Reichskanzlei

K210400

372024

d. II. 29. s. Ro.

Stamp: Top Secret

30 copies
16th copy

Minutes of discussion.

I. The following persons took part in the discussion about the final solution of the Jewish question which took place in Berlin, AM Grossen Wannsee No. 56/58 on 20 January 1942.

Gauleiter Dr. Meyer and Reichsamt-leiter Dr. Leibbrand	Reich Ministry for the Occupied Eastern territories
Secretary of State Dr. Stuckart	Reich Ministry for the Interior
Secretary of State Neumann	Plenipotentiary for the Four Year Plan
Secretary of State Dr. Freisler	Reich Ministry of Justice
Secretary of State Dr. Buehle	Office of the Government General
Under Secretary of State Dr. Luther	Foreign Office
SS-Oberfuhrer Klopfer	Party Chancellery
Ministerialdirektor Kritzinger	Reich Chancellery

LEFT AND FOLLOWING PAGES The minutes of the Wannsee Conference, written by Eichmann, approved by Heydrich, were deliberately opaque, with euphemisms – the term "Final Solution" itself, for example – throughout. Circulation was tightly controlled: 30 copies were made; only one survives.

- 2 -

SS-Gruppenführer Hofmann   Rasse- und Siedlungs-hauptamt

SS-Gruppenführer Müller   Reichssicherheits-hauptamt
SS-Obersturmbannführer Eichmann

SS-Oberführer Dr. Schöngarth   Sicherheitspolizei
Befehlshaber der Sicherheits-   und SD
polizei und des SD im Generalgouvernement

SS-Sturmbannführer Dr. Lange   Sicherheitspolizei
Kommandeur der Sicherheitspoli-   und SD
zei und des SD für den General-
bezirk Lettland, als Vertreter
des Befehlshabers der Sicherheitspolizei und des SD für das
Reichskommissariat Ostland.

II.   Chef der Sicherheitspolizei und des SD,
SS-Obergruppenführer H e y d r i c h , teilte
eingangs seine Bestellung zum Beauftragten für die
Vorbereitung der Endlösung der europäischen Judenfrage durch den Reichsmarschall mit und wies darauf hin, daß zu dieser Besprechung geladen wurde,
um Klarheit in grundsätzlichen Fragen zu schaffen.
Der Wunsch des Reichsmarschalls, ihm einen Ent-
wurf über die organisatorischen, sachlichen und
materiellen Belange im Hinblick auf die Endlösung
der europäischen Judenfrage zu übersenden, erfor-
dert die vorherige gemeinsame Behandlung aller
an diesen Fragen unmittelbar beteiligten Zentral-
instanzen im Hinblick auf die Parallelisierung
der Linienführung.

K210401   372025

SS-Gruppenfuehrer Hofmann	Race and Settlement Main Office
SS-Gruppenfuehrer Mueller	Reich Main Security Office
SS-Obersturmbannfuehrer Eichmann	
SS-Oberfuehrer Dr. Schoengarth Chief of the Security Police and the SD in the Government General	Security Police and SD
SS-Sturmbannfuehrer Dr. Lange Commander of the Security Police and the SD for the General-District Latvia, as deputy of the Commander of the Security Police and the SD for the Reich Commissariat "Eastland".	Security Police and SD

II.   At the beginning of the discussion Chief of the Security Police and of the SD, SS-Obergruppenfuehrer Heydrich, reported that the Reich Marshal had appointed him delegate for the preparations for the final solution of the Jewish question in Europe and pointed out that this discussion had been called for the purpose of clarifying fundamental questions. The wish of the Reich Marshal to have a draft sent to him concerning organizational, factual and material interests in relation to the final solution of the Jewish question in Europe makes necessary an initial common action of all central offices immediately concerned with these questions in order to bring their general activities into line.

168

- 3 -

Die Federführung bei der Bearbeitung der
Endlösung der Judenfrage liege ohne Rücksicht auf
geographische Grenzen zentral beim Reichsführer-ϟϟ
und Chef der Deutschen Polizei (Chef der Sicherheitspolizei und des SD).

Der Chef der Sicherheitspolizei und des
SD gab sodann einen kurzen Rückblick über den bis-
her geführten Kampf gegen diesen Gegner. Die we-
sentlichsten Momente bilden

a/ die Zurückdrängung der Juden aus den
   einzelnen Lebensgebieten des deutschen Volkes,

b/ die Zurückdrängung der Juden aus dem
   Lebensraum des deutschen Volkes.

Im Vollzug dieser Bestrebungen wurde als
einzige vorläufige Lösungsmöglichkeit die Beschleu-
nigung der Auswanderung der Juden aus dem Reichsgebiet verstärkt und planmäßig in Angriff genommen.

Auf Anordnung des Reichsmarschalls wurde
im Januar 1939 eine Reichszentrale für jüdische Auswanderung errichtet, mit deren Leitung der Chef der
Sicherheitspolizei und des SD betraut wurde. Sie
hatte insbesondere die Aufgabe

a/ alle Maßnahmen zur Vorbereitung einer
   verstärkten Auswanderung der Juden zu
   treffen,

b/ den Auswanderungsstrom zu lenken,

c/ die Durchführung der Auswanderung im
   Einzelfall zu beschleunigen.

Das Aufgabenziel war, auf legale Weise
den deutschen Lebensraum von Juden zu säubern.

K210402   372026

The Reichsfuehrer-SS and the Chief of the German Police (Chief of the Security Police and the SD) were entrusted with the official central handling of the final solution of the Jewish question without regard to geographic borders.

The Chief of the Security Police and the SD then gave a short report of the struggle which has been carried on thus far against this enemy, the essential points being the following:

a) the expulsion of the Jews from every sphere of life of the German people,

b) the expulsion of the Jews from the living space of the German people.

In carrying out these efforts, an increased and planned acceleration of the emigration of the Jews from Reich territory was started, as the only possible present solution.

By order of the Reich Marshal, a Reich Central Office for Jewish Emigration was set up in January 1939 and the Chief of the Security Police and SD was entrusted with the management. Its most important tasks were

a) to make all necessary arrangements for the preparation for an increased emigration of the Jews,

b) to direct the flow of emigration,

c) to speed the procedure of emigration in each individual case.

The aim of all this was to cleanse German living space of Jews in a legal manner.

- 4 -

Über die Nachteile, die eine solche Aus-
wanderungsforcierung mit sich brachte, waren sich
alle Stellen im klaren. Sie mußten jedoch ange-
sichts des Fehlens anderer Lösungsmöglichkeiten
vorerst in Kauf genommen werden.

Die Auswanderungsarbeiten waren in der
Folgezeit nicht nur ein deutsches Problem, sondern auch ein Problem, mit dem sich die Behörden
der Ziel- bzw. Einwandererländer zu befassen hat-
ten. Die finanziellen Schwierigkeiten, wie Erhö-
hung der Vorzeige- und Landungsgelder seitens
der verschiedenen ausländischen Regierungen, feh-
lende Schiffsplätze, laufend verschärfte Einwan-
derungsbeschränkungen oder -sperren, erschwerten
die Auswanderungsbestrebungen außerordentlich.
Trotz dieser Schwierigkeiten wurden seit der
Machtübernahme bis zum Stichtag 31.10.1941 insgesamt rund 537.000 Juden zur Auswanderung ge-
bracht. Davon

vom 30.1.1933 aus dem Altreich   rd. 360.000
vom 15.3.1938 aus der Ostmark   rd. 147.000
vom 15.3.1939 aus dem Protektorat
            Böhmen und Mähren   rd. 30.000.

Die Finanzierung der Auswanderung erfolg-
te durch die Juden bzw. jüdisch-politischen Organisationen selbst. Um den Verbleib der verproleta-
risierten Juden zu vermeiden, wurde nach dem Grund-
satz verfahren, daß die vermögenden Juden die Abwanderung der vermögenslosen Juden zu finanzieren
haben; hier wurde, je nach Vermögen gestaffelt,
eine entsprechende Umlage bzw. Auswandererabgabe
vorgeschrieben, die zur Bestreitung der finanziellen Obliegenheiten im Zuge der Abwanderung vermö-
gensloser Juden verwandt wurde.

K210403   372027

All the officers realized the drawbacks of such enforced accelerated emigration. For the time being they had, however, tolerated it on account of the lack of other possible solutions to the problem.

The work concerned with emigration was, later on, not only a German problem, but also a problem with which the authorities of the countries to which the flow of emigrants was being directed would have to deal. Financial difficulties, such as the demand by various foreign governments for increasing sums of money to be presented at the time of the landing, the lack of shipping space, increasing restriction of entry permits, or the cancelling of such, increased extraordinarily the difficulties of emigration. In spite of these difficulties, 537,000 Jews were sent out of the country between the takeover of power and the deadline of 31 October 1941. Of these

approximately 360,000 were in Germany proper on 30 January 1933

approximately 147,000 were in Austria (Ostmark) on 15 March 1939

approximately 30,000 were in the Protectorate of Bohemia and Moravia on 15 March 1939.

The Jews themselves, or their Jewish political organizations, financed the emigration. In order to avoid impoverished Jews remaining behind, the principle was followed that wealthy Jews have to finance the emigration of poor Jews; this was arranged by imposing a suitable tax, i.e., an emigration tax, which was used for financial arrangements in connection with the emigration of poor Jews and was imposed according to income.

- 5 -

Neben dem Reichsmark-Aufkommen sind Devisen für Vorzeige- und Landungsgelder erforderlich gewesen. Um den deutschen Devisenschatz zu schonen, wurden die jüdischen Finanzinstitutionen des Auslandes durch die jüdischen Organisationen des Inlandes verhalten, für die Beitreibung entsprechender Devisenaufkommen Sorge zu tragen. Hier wurden durch diese ausländischen Juden im Schenkungswege bis zum 30.10.1941 insgesamt rund 9.500.000 Dollar zur Verfügung gestellt.

Inzwischen hat der Reichsführer-SS und Chef der Deutschen Polizei im Hinblick auf die Gefahren einer Auswanderung im Kriege und im Hinblick auf die Möglichkeiten des Ostens die Auswanderung von Juden verboten.

III.   Anstelle der Auswanderung ist nunmehr als weitere Lösungsmöglichkeit nach entsprechender vorheriger Genehmigung durch den Führer die Evakuierung der Juden nach dem Osten getreten.

Diese Aktionen sind jedoch lediglich als Ausweichmöglichkeiten anzusprechen, doch werden hier bereits jene praktischen Erfahrungen gesammelt, die im Hinblick auf die kommende Endlösung der Judenfrage von wichtiger Bedeutung sind.

Im Zuge dieser Endlösung der europäischen Judenfrage kommen rund 11 Millionen Juden in Betracht, die sich wie folgt auf die einzelnen Länder verteilen:

K210404

Apart from the necessary Reichsmark exchange, foreign currency had to be presented at the time of landing. In order to save foreign exchange held by Germany, the foreign Jewish financial organizations were – with the help of Jewish organizations in Germany – made responsible for arranging an adequate amount of foreign currency. Up to 30 October 1941, these foreign Jews donated a total of around 9,500,000 dollars.

In the meantime the Reichsfuehrer-SS and Chief of the German Police had prohibited emigration of Jews due to the dangers of an emigration in wartime and due to the possibilities of the East.

III.   Another possible solution to the problem has now taken the place of emigration, i.e. the evacuation of the Jews to the East, provided that the Fuehrer gives the appropriate approval in advance.

These actions are, however, only to be considered provisional, but practical experience is already being collected which is of the greatest importance in relation to the future final solution of the Jewish question.

Approximately 11 million Jews will be involved in the final solution of the European Jewish question, distributed as follows among the individual countries:

– 6 –

Land	Zahl
A. Altreich	131.800
Ostmark	43.700
Ostgebiete	420.000
Generalgouvernement	2.284.000
Bialystok	400.000
Protektorat Böhmen und Mähren	74.200
Estland – judenfrei –	
Lettland	3.500
Litauen	34.000
Belgien	43.000
Dänemark	5.600
Frankreich / Besetztes Gebiet	165.000
Unbesetztes Gebiet	700.000
Griechenland	69.600
Niederlande	160.800
Norwegen	1.300
B. Bulgarien	48.000
England	330.000
Finnland	2.300
Irland	4.000
Italien einschl. Sardinien	58.000
Albanien	200
Kroatien	40.000
Portugal	3.000
Rumänien.einschl. Bessarabien	342.000
Schweden	8.000
Schweiz	18.000
Serbien	10.000
Slowakei	88.000
Spanien	6.000
Türkei (europ. Teil)	55.500
Ungarn	742.800
UdSSR	5.000.000
Ukraine 2.994.684	
Weißrußland aus-	
schl. Bialystok 446.484	
Zusammen: über	11.000.000

K210405   372029

Country	Number
A. Germany proper	131,800
Austria	43,700
Eastern territories	420,000
General Government	2,284,000
Bialystok	400,000
Protectorate Bohemia and Moravia	74,200
Estonia	
– free of Jews –	
Latvia	3,500
Lithuania	34,000
Belgium	43,000
Denmark	5,600
France / occupied territory	165,000
unoccupied territory	700,000
Greece	69,600
Netherlands	160,800
Norway	1,300
B. Bulgaria	48,000
England	330,000
Finland	2,300
Ireland	4,000
Italy including Sardinia	58,000
Albania	200
Croatia	40,000
Portugal	3,000
Rumania including Bessarabia	342,000
Sweden	8,000
Switzerland	18,000
Serbia	10,000
Slovakia	88,000
Spain	6,000
Turkey (European portion)	55,500
Hungary	742,800
USSR	5,000,000
Ukraine	2,994,684
White Russia	
excluding Bialystok	446,484
Total over	11,000,000

- 7 -

Bei den angegebenen Judenzahlen der verschiedenen ausländischen Staaten handelt es sich
jedoch nur um Glaubensjuden, da die Begriffsbe-
stimmungen der Juden nach rassischen Grundsätzen
teilweise dort noch fehlen. Die Behandlung des
Problems in den einzelnen Ländern wird im Hinblick
auf die allgemeine Haltung und Auffassung auf gewisse Schwierigkeiten stoßen, besonders in Ungarn
und Rumänien. So kann sich z.B. heute noch in Rumänien der Jude gegen Geld entsprechende Dokumen-
te, die ihm eine fremde Staatsangehörigkeit amt-
lich bescheinigen, beschaffen.

Der Einfluß der Juden auf alle Gebiete
in der UdSSR ist bekannt. Im europäischen Gebiet
leben etwa 5 Millionen, im asiatischen Raum knapp
1/4 Million Juden.

Die berufsständische Aufgliederung der
im europäischen Gebiet der UdSSR ansässigen Juden
war etwa folgende:

In der Landwirtschaft	9,1 %
als städtische Arbeiter	14,8 %
im Handel	20,0 %
als Staatsarbeiter angestellt	23,4 %
in den privaten Berufen – Heilkunde, Presse, Theater, usw.	32,7 %

Unter entsprechender Leitung sollen nun
im Zuge der Endlösung die Juden in geeigneter Weise im Osten zum Arbeitseinsatz kommen. In großen
Arbeitskolonnen, unter Trennung der Geschlechter,
werden die arbeitsfähigen Juden straßenbauend in
diese Gebiete geführt, wobei zweifellos ein Groß-
teil durch natürliche Verminderung ausfallen wird

K210406   372030

The number of Jews given here for foreign countries includes, however, only those Jews who still adhere to the Jewish faith, since some countries still do not have a definition of the term "Jew" according to racial principles.

The handling of the problem in the individual countries will meet with difficulties due to the attitude and outlook of the people there, especially in Hungary and Rumania. Thus, for example, even today the Jew can buy documents in Rumania that will officially prove his foreign citizenship.

The influence of the Jews in all walks of life in the USSR is well known. Approximately five million Jews live in the European part of the USSR, in the Asian part scarcely 1/4 million.

The breakdown of Jews residing in the European part of the USSR according to trades was approximately as follows:

Agriculture	9.1 %
Urban workers	14.8 %
In trade	20.0 %
Employed by the state	23.4 %
In private occupations such as medical profession, press, theater, etc.	32. 7%

Under proper guidance, in the course of the final solution the Jews are to be allocated for appropriate labor in the East. Able-bodied Jews, separated according to sex, will be taken in large work columns to these areas for work on roads, in the course of which action doubtless a large portion will be eliminated by natural causes.

173

- 8 -

Der allfällig endlich verbleibende Rest-
bestand wird, da es sich bei diesem zweifellos um
den widerstandsfähigsten Teil handelt, entsprechend
behandelt werden müssen, da dieser, eine natürliche
Auslese darstellend, bei Freilassung als Keimzelle
eines neuen jüdischen Aufbaues anzusprechen ist.
(Siehe die Erfahrung der Geschichte.)

Im Zuge der praktischen Durchführung der
Endlösung wird Europa vom Westen nach Osten durch-
gekämmt. Das Reichsgebiet einschließlich Protektorat Böhmen und Mähren wird, allein schon aus Grün-
den der Wohnungsfrage und sonstigen sozial-politi-
schen Notwendigkeiten, vorweggenommen werden müssen.

Die evakuierten Juden werden zunächst Zug
um Zug in sogenannte Durchgangsghettos verbracht,
um von dort aus weiter nach dem Osten transportiert
zu werden.

Wichtige Voraussetzung, so führte ₰-Ober-
gruppenführer H e y d r i c h weiter aus, für die
Durchführung der Evakuierung überhaupt, ist die ge-
naue Festlegung des in Betracht kommenden Personen-
kreises.

Es ist beabsichtigt, Juden im Alter von
über 65 Jahren nicht zu evakuieren, sondern sie einem Altersghetto - vorgesehen ist Theresienstadt -
zu überstellen.

Neben diesen Altersklassen - von den am
31.10.1941 sich im Altreich und der Ostmark befind-
lichen etwa 280.000 Juden sind etwa 30 % über 65 Jah-
re alt - finden in den jüdischen Altersghettos weiterhin die schwerkriegsbeschädigten Juden und Juden
mit Kriegsauszeichnungen (EK I) Aufnahme. Mit dieser

K210407   372031

The possible final remnant will, since it will undoubtedly consist of the most resistant portion, have to be treated accordingly, because it is the product of natural selection and would, if released, act as a the seed of a new Jewish revival (see the experience of history.)

In the course of the practical execution of the final solution, Europe will be combed through from west to east. Germany proper, including the Protectorate of Bohemia and Moravia, will have to be handled first due to the housing problem and additional social and political necessities.

The evacuated Jews will first be sent, group by group, to so-called transit ghettos, from which they will be transported to the East.

SS-Obergruppenfuehrer Heydrich went on to say that an important prerequisite for the evacuation as such is the exact definition of the persons involved.

It is not intended to evacuate Jews over 65 years old, but to send them to an old-age ghetto – Theresienstadt is being considered for this purpose.

In addition to these age groups – of the approximately 280,000 Jews in Germany proper and Austria on 31 October 1941, approximately 30% are over 65 years old – severely wounded veterans and Jews with war decorations (Iron Cross I) will be

– 9 –

zweckmäßigen Lösung werden mit einem Schlag die
vielen Interventionen ausgeschaltet.

Der Beginn der einzelnen größeren Evakuierungsaktionen wird weitgehend von der militäri-
schen Entwicklung abhängig sein. Bezüglich der Behandlung der Endlösung in den von uns besetzten und
beeinflußten europäischen Gebieten wurde vorgeschla-
gen, daß die in Betracht kommenden Sachbearbeiter
des Auswärtigen Amtes sich mit dem zuständigen Re-
ferenten der Sicherheitspolizei und des SD bespre-
chen.

In der Slowakei und Kroatien ist die Angelegenheit nicht mehr allzu schwer, da die wesentlich-
sten Kernfragen in dieser Hinsicht dort bereits einer Lösung zugeführt wurden. In Rumänien hat die Regierung inzwischen ebenfalls einen Judenbeauftragten
eingesetzt. Zur Regelung der Frage in Ungarn ist es
erforderlich, in Zeitkürze einen Berater für Juden-
fragen der Ungarischen Regierung aufzuoktroyieren.

Hinsichtlich der Aufnahme der Vorbereitun-
gen zur Regelung des Problems in Italien hält M-Ober-
gruppenführer H e y d r i c h eine Verbindung zum
Polizei-Chef in diesen Belangen für angebracht.

Im besetzten und unbesetzten Frankreich
wird die Erfassung der Juden zur Evakuierung aller
Wahrscheinlichkeit nach ohne große Schwierigkeiten
vor sich gehen können.

Unterstaatssekretär L u t h e r teilte
hierzu mit, daß bei tiefgehender Behandlung dieses
Problems in einigen Ländern, so in den nordischen
Staaten, Schwierigkeiten auftauchen werden, und es
sich daher empfiehlt, diese Länder vorerst noch zu-

K210408

372032

accepted in the old-age ghettos. With this expedient solution, in one fell swoop many interventions will be prevented.

The beginning of the individual larger evacuation actions will largely depend on military developments. Regarding the handling of the final solution in those European countries occupied and influenced by us, it was proposed that the appropriate expert of the Foreign Office discuss the matter with the responsible official of the Security Police and SD.

In Slovakia and Croatia the matter is no longer so difficult, since the most substantial problems in this respect have already been brought near a solution. In Rumania the government has in the meantime also appointed a commissioner for Jewish affairs. In order to settle the question in Hungary, it will soon be necessary to force an adviser for Jewish questions onto the Hungarian government.

With regard to taking up preparations for dealing with the problem in Italy, SS-Obergruppenfuehrer Heydrich considers it opportune to contact the chief of police with a view to these problems.

In occupied and unoccupied France, the registration of Jews for evacuation will in all probability proceed without great difficulty.

Under Secretary of State Luther calls attention in this matter to the fact that in some countries, such as the Scandinavian states, difficulties will arise if this problem is dealt with thoroughly and that it will therefore be advisable to defer actions in these countries. Besides, in view of the small

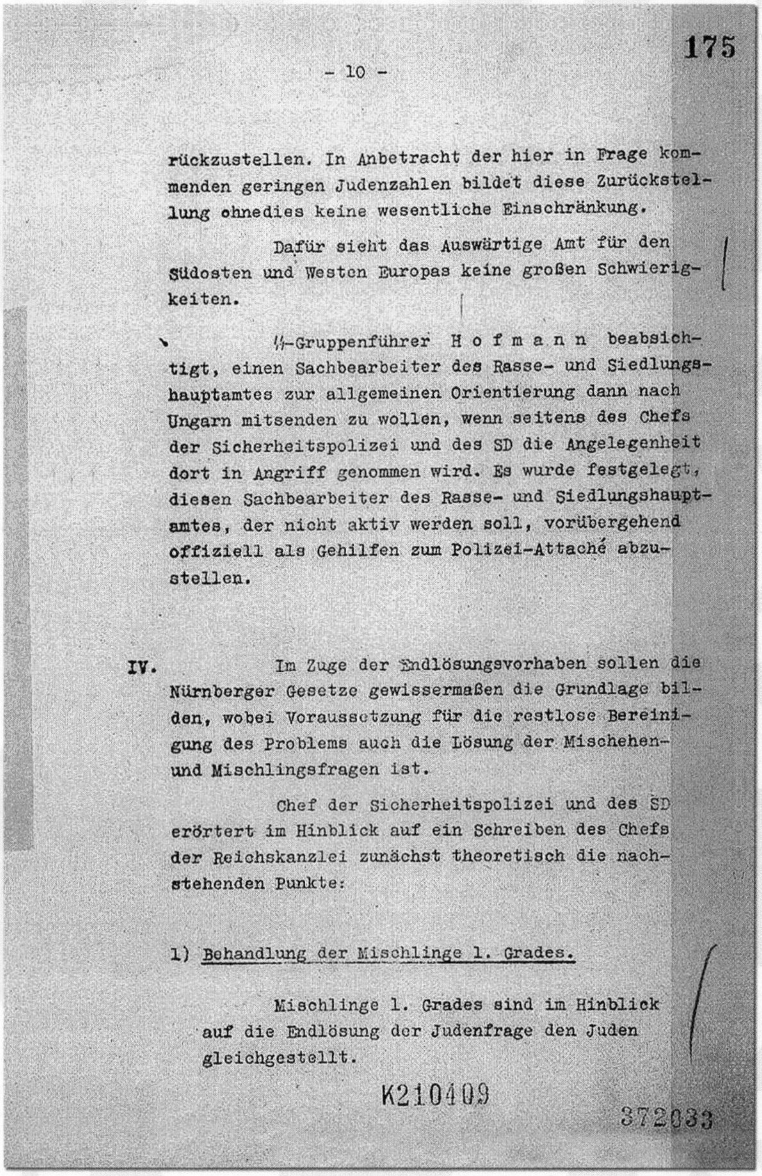

175

\- 10 -

rückzustellen. In Anbetracht der hier in Frage kommenden geringen Judenzahlen bildet diese Zurückstellung ohnedies keine wesentliche Einschränkung.

Dafür sieht das Auswärtige Amt für den Südosten und Westen Europas keine großen Schwierigkeiten.

SS-Gruppenführer H o f m a n n beabsichtigt, einen Sachbearbeiter des Rasse- und Siedlungshauptamtes zur allgemeinen Orientierung dann nach Ungarn mitsenden zu wollen, wenn seitens des Chefs der Sicherheitspolizei und des SD die Angelegenheit dort in Angriff genommen wird. Es wurde festgelegt, diesen Sachbearbeiter des Rasse- und Siedlungshauptamtes, der nicht aktiv werden soll, vorübergehend offiziell als Gehilfen zum Polizei-Attaché abzustellen.

IV. Im Zuge der Endlösungsvorhaben sollen die Nürnberger Gesetze gewissermaßen die Grundlage bilden, wobei Voraussetzung für die restlose Bereinigung des Problems auch die Lösung der Mischehen- und Mischlingsfragen ist.

Chef der Sicherheitspolizei und des SD erörtert im Hinblick auf ein Schreiben des Chefs der Reichskanzlei zunächst theoretisch die nachstehenden Punkte:

1) Behandlung der Mischlinge 1. Grades.

Mischlinge 1. Grades sind im Hinblick auf die Endlösung der Judenfrage den Juden gleichgestellt.

K210409

372033

numbers of Jews affected, this deferral will not cause any substantial limitation.

The Foreign Office sees no great difficulties for southeast and western Europe.

SS-Gruppenfuehrer Hofmann plans to send an expert to Hungary from the Race and Settlement Main Office for general orientation at the time when the Chief of the Security Police and SD takes up the matter there. It was decided to assign this expert from the Race and Settlement Main Office, who will not work actively, as an assistant to the police attache.

IV. In the course of the final solution plans, the Nuremberg Laws should provide a certain foundation, in which a prerequisite for the absolute solution of the problem is also the solution to the problem of mixed marriages and persons of mixed blood.

The Chief of the Security Police and the SD discusses the following points, at first theoretically, in regard to a letter from the chief of the Reich chancellery:

1) Treatment of Persons of Mixed Blood of the First Degree

Persons of mixed blood of the first degree will, as regards the final solution of the Jewish question, be treated as Jews.

From this treatment the following exceptions will be made:

a) Persons of mixed blood of the first degree married to persons of German blood if their marriage has resulted in children (persons of mixed blood of the second degree). These persons of mixed blood of the second degree are to be treated essentially as Germans.

b) Persons of mixed blood of the first degree, for whom the highest offices of the Party and State have already issued exemption permits in any sphere of life. Each individual case must be examined, and it is not ruled out that the decision may be made to the detriment of the person of mixed blood.

The prerequisite for any exemption must always be the personal merit of the person of mixed blood. (Not the merit of the parent or spouse of German blood.)

Persons of mixed blood of the first degree who are exempted from evacuation will be sterilized in order to prevent any offspring and to eliminate the problem of persons of mixed blood once and for all. Such sterilization will be voluntary. But it is required to remain in the Reich. The sterilized "person of mixed blood" is thereafter free of all restrictions to which he was previously subjected.

2) Treatment of Persons of Mixed Blood of the Second Degree

Persons of mixed blood of the second degree will be treated fundamentally as persons of German blood, with the exception of the following cases, in which the persons of mixed blood of the second degree will be considered as Jews:

- 12 -

a) Herkunft des Mischlings 2. Grades
aus einer Bastardehe (beide Teile
Mischlinge).

b) Rassisch besonders ungünstiges Er-
scheinungsbild des Mischlings 2.
Grades, das ihn schon äußerlich
zu den Juden rechnet.

c) Besonders schlechte polizeiliche
und politische Beurteilung des
Mischlings 2. Grades, die erken-
nen läßt, daß er sich wie ein Jude fühlt und benimmt.

Auch in diesen Fällen sollen aber dann
Ausnahmen nicht gemacht werden, wenn der Mischling 2. Grades deutschblütig verheiratet ist.

3) Ehen zwischen Volljuden und Deutschblütigen.

Von Einzelfall zu Einzelfall muß hier
entschieden werden, ob der jüdische Teil evakuiert wird, oder ob er unter Berücksichtigung
auf die Auswirkungen einer solchen Maßnahme
auf die deutschen Verwandten dieser Mischehe
einem Altersghetto überstellt wird.

4) Ehen zwischen Mischlingen 1. Grades und
Deutschblütigen.

a) Ohne Kinder.

Sind aus der Ehe keine Kinder hervorgegangen, wird der Mischling 1. Grades
evakuiert bzw. einem Altersghetto überstellt. (Gleiche Behandlung wie bei Ehen
zwischen Volljuden und Deutschblütigen,
Punkt 3.)

K210411

372035

a) The person of mixed blood of the second
degree was born of a marriage in which both
parents are persons of mixed blood.

b) The person of mixed blood of the second
degree has a racially especially undesirable
appearance that marks him outwardly
as a Jew.

c) The person of mixed blood of the second
degree has a particularly bad police and
political record that shows that he feels and
behaves like a Jew.

Also in these cases exemptions should not be made
if the person of mixed blood of the second degree has
married a person of German blood.

3) Marriages between Full Jews and Persons of
German Blood.

Here it must be decided from case to case whether
the Jewish partner will be evacuated or whether, with
regard to the effects of such a step on the German
relatives, [this mixed marriage] should be sent to
an old-age ghetto.

4) Marriages between Persons of Mixed Blood of the
First Degree and Persons of German Blood.

a) Without Children.

If no children have resulted from the
marriage, the person of mixed blood of the
first degree will be evacuated or sent to an
old-age ghetto (same treatments in the case
of marriages between full Jews and persons
of German blood, point 3.)

178

- 13 -

b) Mit Kindern.

Sind Kinder aus der Ehe hervorgegangen
(Mischlinge 2. Grades), werden sie,
wenn sie den Juden gleichgestellt werden, zusammen mit dem Mischling 1. Grades evakuiert bzw. einem Ghetto überstellt. Soweit diese Kinder Deutschen
gleichgestellt werden (Regelfälle),
sind sie von der Evakuierung auszunehm-
men und damit auch der Mischling 1. Grades.

5) Ehen zwischen Mischlingen 1. Grades und Mischlingen 1. Grades oder Juden.

Bei diesen Ehen (einschließlich der Kinder) werden alle Teile wie Juden behandelt und
daher evakuiert bzw. einem Altersghetto überstellt.

6) Ehen zwischen Mischlingen 1. Grades und Mischlingen 2. Grades.

Beide Eheteile werden ohne Rücksicht darauf, ob Kinder vorhanden sind oder nicht, evakuiert bzw. einem Altersghetto überstellt, da et-
waige Kinder rassenmäßig in der Regel einen stär-
keren jüdischen Bluteinschlag aufweisen, als die
jüdischen Mischlinge 2. Grade)

SS-Gruppenführer H o f m a n n steht auf
dem Standpunkt, daß von der Sterilisierung weitgehend Gebrauch gemacht werden muß; zumal der Misch-

K210412   372036

b) With Children.

If children have resulted from the marriage
(persons of mixed blood of the second
degree), they will, if they are to be treated
as Jews, be evacuated or sent to a ghetto
along with the parent of mixed blood
of the first degree. If these children are
to be treated as Germans (regular cases),
they are exempted from evacuation as is
therefore the parent of mixed blood of the
first degree.

5) Marriages between Persons of Mixed Blood of
the First Degree and Persons of Mixed Blood
of the First Degree or Jews. In these marriages
(including the children) all members of the family
will be treated as Jews and therefore be evacuated
or sent to an old-age ghetto.

6) Marriages between Persons of Mixed Blood of
the First Degree and Persons of Mixed Blood
of the Second Degree.

In these marriages both partners will be evacuated
or sent to an old-age ghetto without consideration of
whether the marriage has produced children, since
possible children will as a

- 14 -

ling, vor die Wahl gestellt, ob er evakuiert oder
sterilisiert werden soll, sich lieber der Sterilisierung unterziehen würde.

Staatssekretär Dr. S t u c k a r t
stellt fest, daß die praktische Durchführung der
eben mitgeteilten Lösungsmöglichkeiten zur Bereinigung der Mischehen- und Mischlingsfragen in dieser Form eine unendliche Verwaltungsarbeit mit
sich bringen würde. Um zum anderen auf alle Fälle
auch den biologischen Tatsachen Rechnung zu tragen,
schlug Staatssekretär Dr. S t u c k a r t vor,
zur Zwangssterilisierung zu schreiten.

Zur Vereinfachung des Mischehenproblems
müßten ferner Möglichkeiten überlegt werden mit
dem Ziel, daß der Gesetzgeber etwa sagt: "Diese
Ehen sind geschieden".

Bezüglich der Frage der Auswirkung der
Judenevakuierung auf das Wirtschaftsleben erklär-
te Staatssekretär N e u m a n n , daß die in
kriegswichtigen Betrieben im Arbeitseinsatz stehen-
den Juden derzeit, solange noch kein Ersatz zur
Verfügung steht, nicht evakuiert werden könnten.

SS-Obergruppenführer H e y d r i c h
wies darauf hin, daß diese Juden nach den von ihm
genehmigten Richtlinien zur Durchführung der derzeit laufenden Evakuierungsaktionen ohnedies nicht
evakuiert würden.

Staatssekretär Dr. B ü h l e r stellte
fest, daß das Generalgouvernement es begrüßen würde, wenn mit der Endlösung dieser Frage im Generalgouvernement begonnen würde, weil einmal hier das
Transportproblem keine übergeordnete Rolle spielt

K210413   372037

---

rule have stronger Jewish blood than the Jewish person of mixed blood of the second degree.

SS-Gruppenfuehrer Hofmann advocates the opinion that sterilization will have to be widely used, since the person of mixed blood who is given the choice whether he will be evacuated or sterilized would rather undergo sterilization.

State Secretary Dr. Stuckart maintains that carrying out in practice of the just mentioned possibilities for solving the problem of mixed marriages and persons of mixed blood will create endless administrative work. In the second place, as the biological facts cannot be disregarded in any case, State Secretary Dr. Stuckart proposed proceeding to forced sterilization.

Furthermore, to simplify the problem of mixed marriages possibilities must be considered with the goal of the legislator saying something like: "These marriages have been dissolved."

With regard to the issue of the effect of the evacuation of Jews on the economy, State Secretary Neumann stated that Jews who are working in industries vital to the war effort, provided that no replacements are available, cannot be evacuated.

SS-Obergruppenfuehrer Heydrich indicated that these Jews would not be evacuated according to the rules he had approved for carrying out the evacuations then underway.

State Secretary Dr. Buehler stated that the General Government would welcome it if the final solution of this problem could be begun in the General Government, since on the one hand transportation does not play such a large role here nor would problems of labor supply hamper this action. Jews must be

und arbeitseinsatzmäßige Gründe den Lauf dieser
Aktion nicht behindern würden. Juden müßten so
schnell wie möglich aus dem Gebiet des Generalgouvernements entfernt werden, weil gerade hier
der Jude als Seuchenträger eine eminente Gefahr
bedeutet und er zum anderen durch fortgesetzten
Schleichhandel die wirtschaftliche Struktur des
Landes dauernd in Unordnung bringt. Von den in
Frage kommenden etwa 2 1/2 Millionen Juden sei
überdies die Mehrzahl der Fälle arbeitsunfähig.

        Staatssekretär Dr. B ü h l e r stellt
weiterhin fest, daß die Lösung der Judenfrage im
Generalgouvernement federführend beim Chef der
Sicherheitspolizei und des SD liegt und seine Arbeiten durch die Behörden des Generalgouvernements
unterstützt würden. Er hätte nur eine Bitte, die
Judenfrage in diesem Gebiet so schnell wie möglich
zu lösen.

        Abschließend wurden die verschiedenen Ar-
ten der Lösungsmöglichkeiten besprochen, wobei so-
wohl seitens des Gauleiters Dr. M e y e r als auch
seitens des Staatssekretärs Dr. B ü h l e r der
Standpunkt vertreten wurde, gewisse vorbereitende
Arbeiten im Zuge der Endlösung gleich in den be-
treffenden Gebieten selbst durchzuführen, wobei
jedoch eine Beunruhigung der Bevölkerung vermieden
werden müsse.

        Mit der Bitte des Chefs der Sicherheits-
polizei und des SD an die Besprechungsteilnehmer,
ihm bei der Durchführung der Lösungsarbeiten entsprechende Unterstützung zu gewähren, wurde die
Besprechung geschlossen.

K210414   372038

removed from the territory of the General Government as quickly as possible, since it is especially here that the Jew as an epidemic carrier represents an extreme danger and on the other hand he is causing permanent chaos in the economic structure of the country through continued black market dealings. Moreover, of the approximately 2½ million Jews concerned, the majority is unfit for work.

State Secretary Dr. Buehler stated further that the solution to the Jewish question in the General Government is the responsibility of the Chief of the Security Police and the SD and that his efforts would be supported by the officials of the General Government. He had only one request, to solve the Jewish question in this area as quickly as possible.

In conclusion the different types of possible solutions were discussed, during which discussion both Gauleiter Dr. Meyer and State Secretary Dr. Buehler took the position that certain preparatory activities for the final solution should be carried out immediately in the territories in question, in which process alarming the populace must be avoided.

The meeting was closed with the request of the Chief of the Security Police and the SD to the participants that they afford him appropriate support during the carrying out of the tasks involved in the solution.

The First Killing Centres

The decision by the Nazis in the autumn of 1941 to eliminate the entirety of Europe's Jews had an obvious drawback: given the difficulties experienced with shooting their victims, no one knew how murder on this scale could be carried out. The goal was the potential death of 11 million. Even the most aggressive of the SS officers charged with the slaughter were unable to imagine any practical means of killing this many people.

By December 1941, a solution of sorts had been suggested: mobile gas chambers, trucks packed with their victims who could be gassed by the machines' re-directed exhausts. Self-evidently, the numbers killed were small, perhaps 50–70 at a time in the smaller trucks, up to 150 in the larger, though the trucks had the advantage that those killed could then be driven directly to discreet places of burial, though unloading them, their victims having turned a livid pink, consistently distressed their SS operators. In fairly short order, slave labourers were given the job. But a new idea had been born: that the most likely way of exterminating the Jews en masse was to gas them.

Trucks of this kind had first been used in September 1941, the victims Soviet mental patients. At much the same time, Zyklon B, developed in Berlin in the early Twenties as a pesticide, was experimented with at Auschwitz, the

victims this time Soviet prisoners of war bundled into the camp's mortuary, converted into a makeshift gas chamber. The screams of the dying were drowned by two motorcycles running at full throttle outside.

It was not until December 1941, before the details of the Final Solution had been agreed, that it became clear that a new kind of camp dedicated to the systematic killing of Jews was required. Chelmno was the first, used to murder Polish Jews deported from what even the Nazis conceded was the dangerously overcrowded ghetto at Lódz, 30 miles

to the southeast. Chelmno never had purpose-built gas chambers: gas trucks were used exclusively until the camp's final destruction by the Nazis in January 1945. An estimated 152,000 perished there.

OPPOSITE The innocent: Jewish children being taken for "resettlement" at Chelmno.

ABOVE More innocents: children in the ghetto at Lódz.

Similarly, hasty improvisation occurred at Auschwitz-Birkenau. By 1943, Birkenau had become synonymous with mass murder on an industrial scale. But in the spring of 1942, the killings were almost literally a cottage industry; two peasant houses – Bunker 1, otherwise known as the Little Red House, and Bunker 2, the Little White House – hurriedly converted into gas chambers. Stop-gap solutions or not, they were strikingly effective. Between March and December 1942, almost 100,000 Polish, French, Dutch, Belgian and Slovak Jews were murdered in these improvised gas chambers.

The killings created a further problem. What to do with the corpses? In time, the answer would be to burn them in a series of vast crematoria. But in the short term, mass graves, dug by Jewish slave labour, seemed the most likely solution. In the winter and spring, this worked well enough; by mid-summer, however, the corpses were liquefying. Precisely those same Jewish slave labourers who had been detailed to dig the graves and bury the corpses were now forced to dig up the putrefying remains and, laboriously, to burn them.

From the start, for the SS, the Final Solution was a matter not of morality but, more prosaically, of logistics. It is a testament to their gruesome dedication that they were able to come up with short-term responses so readily before more permanent solutions were in place.

OPPOSITE Perhaps one of the most haunting images of the Holocaust, a hazy, illicitly taken photograph of Sonderkommando burning bodies at Auschwitz in the summer of 1943. The film was smuggled from the camp in a toothpaste tube.

BELOW What remains of Bunker 2 – the Little White House – at Auschwitz. Nothing remains of Bunker 1.

The Commandant: Rudolf Höss

For much of its existence, the Commandant at Auschwitz was Rudolf Höss (1900–47), an SS officer since 1934 who the same year was posted to Dachau, Germany's first concentration camp. In May 1940, he was made Commandant of Auschwitz, then a dilapidated former Polish army barracks, charged initially with turning it into a prison camp. After testifying at the Nuremberg, Trials, he was handed over to the Polish authorities. His trial was held in Warsaw. Found guilty, he was sentenced to death, and hanged in the grounds of Auschwitz.

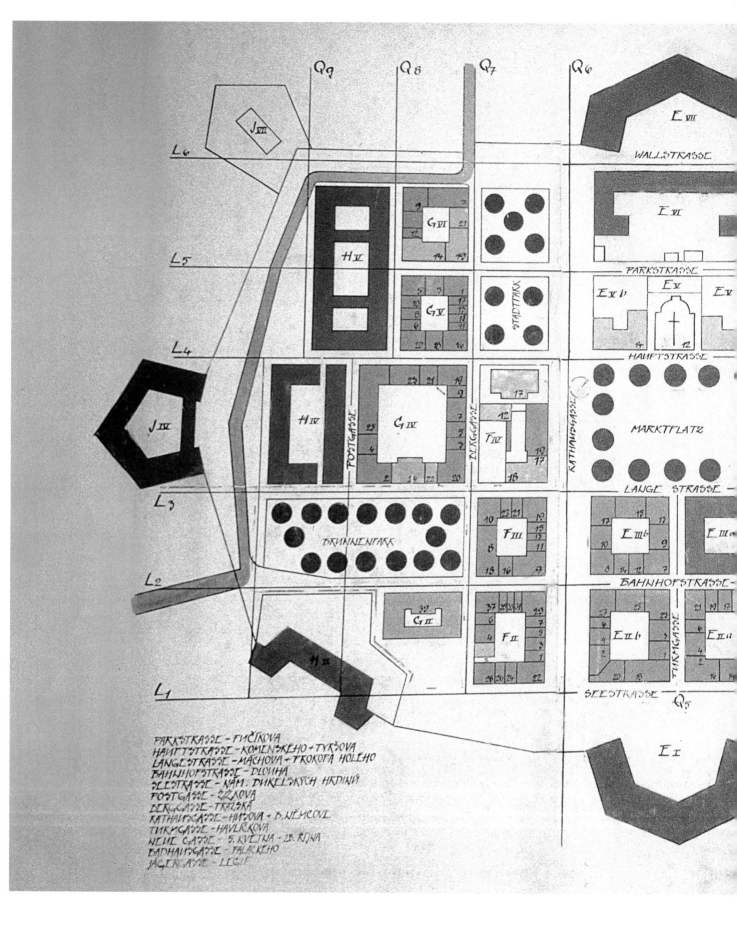

Q_9 Q_8 Q_7 Q_6

J_{VII}

L_6

WALLSTRASSE

E_{VII}

E_{VI}

H_{VI} G_{VII}

L_5

PARKSTRASSE

G_V STADTPARK

E_Xb E_X E_X

L_4

HAUPTSTRASSE

J_{IV} H_{IV} POSTGASSE G_{IV} DENGGASSE F_{IV} KATHAUSGASSE MARKTPLATZ

L_3

LANGE STRASSE

BRUNNENPARK F_{III} E_{IIIb} E_{IIIa}

L_2

BAHNHOFSTRASSE

G_{II} F_{II} E_{IIb} TURKGASSE E_{IIa}

H_{II}

L_1 SEESTRASSE Q_5

E_I

PARKSTRASSE - FUČÍKOVA
HAUPTSTRASSE - KOMENSKÉHO + TYRŠOVA
LANGESTRASSE - MÁCHOVA + PROKOPA HOLÉHO
BAHNHOFSTRASSE - DLOUHA
SEESTRASSE - NÁM. DUKELSKÝCH HRDINŮ
POSTGASSE - ŽIŽKOVA
BERGGASSE - TRŽSKÁ
RATHAUSGASSE - HUSOVA + B.NĚMCOVÉ
TURKGASSE - HAVLÍČKOVA
NEUE GASSE - 5. KVĚTNA + 28. ŘÍJNA
BADHAUSGASSE - PALACKÉHO
JÄGERGASSE - LEGIÍ

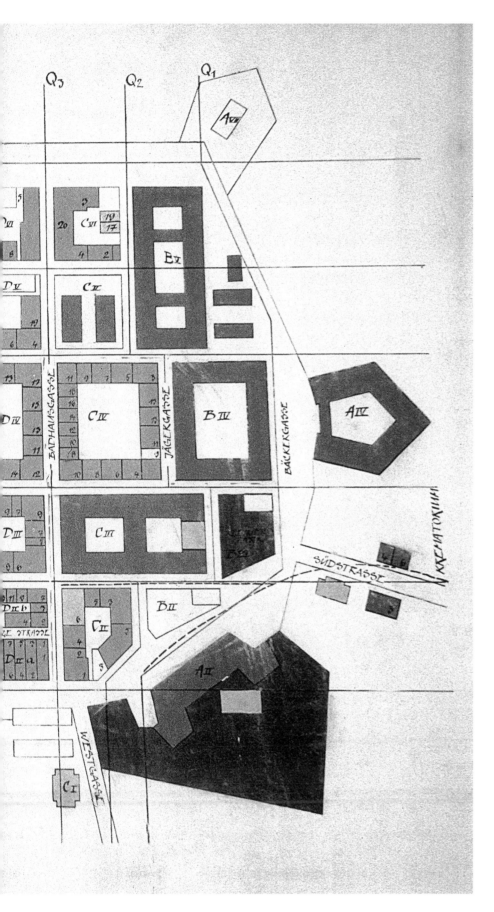

LEFT *A plan of the concentration camp at* Theresienstadt. *The 18th-century Bohemian fortress of Terezín,* Theresienstadt *in German, shown here in a plan from the war, was used as a concentration camp and holding camp for mostly Czech Jews and elderly or otherwise distinguished German and Austrian Jews. At its peak, 60,000 were held in barracks designed for 7,000.*

Trains and Cattle Cars:
Eichmann's Triumph

Without railways, there could have been no Final Solution. Their role was central. All those slaughtered travelled by rail. As such, not merely the German railway company, Deutsche Reichsbahn, but railways companies across Europe played a pivotal part in the death toll. As tellingly, those transported were forced into conditions of extreme squalor, crushed into freight cars for journeys that generally lasted days, trundling towards their inevitable fate.

The man who made it possible was Heydrich's deputy, Adolf Eichmann, a lieutenant-colonel in the SS, charged with Jewish affairs at the Reich Main Security Office. If his organizational abilities were undoubted, his subsequent inability to recognize what they meant in human terms was no less startling. Seized in Argentina in 1960 by Israeli special forces and brought to trial in a blaze of global publicity, his defence consisted of little more than a persistent plea of following orders.

All the Nazi killing centres were on railway lines. Auschwitz stood at the junction of three. The Final Solution now having been definitively decided upon, operations were launched across Nazi-occupied Europe to deport the Jews to the killing centres. Treblinka, Sobibor and Belzec were designated for the murder of the Polish Jews of the General Government. Auschwitz, meanwhile, was assigned to the task of killing Jews from the rest of the continent.

The problems were plain. First, the numbers to be transported were so great, further pressure was placed on the rail system at exactly the moment it was already under immense strain to transport troops and arms to and from the Eastern front. (Between November 1942 and February 1943, the need to give priority to the Eastern Front meant the deportations were stopped altogether.)

That said, even if the number of trains used to transport the Jews was comparatively small, typically no more than one or two a day – it took only 75 trains to transport 75,000 Jews from France, for example, and only 142 trains to transport 437,000 Hungarian Jews in 1944 – their planning still represented a substantial logistical triumph. Throughout, Nazis cynically attempted to persuade their victims not that they were being transported to their deaths but that they were being "resettled" in camps to the east.

OPPOSITE A rare colour photograph of Jews being deported from the Lódz ghetto to Auschwitz, July 1944.

ABOVE Glimpses of freedom: four faces peer through the crude opening of a cattle truck festooned with barbed wire.

Wooden freight cars, *Güterwagen*, typically 9m (30ft) long, were used to transport them. For the Germans, they had the obvious advantages of being cheap and robust. They could also be locked from the outside. Typically, on a train of 60 cars, 100-plus people would be crammed into each car, 6,000 per train, sometimes more. Ventilation came from a small slit. No food or water was provided. There might be a bucket as a lavatory, though there was no means of emptying it. In winter, the Jews shivered and starved; in summer, they sweltered and starved. On occasion, up to 20 per cent died before reaching their destination. The trains travelled at an average speed of about 25kmph (15mph).

On arrival at Treblinka, Sobibor and Belzec, the trains would be split to avoid too many of their passengers disembarking at the same time before being taken to their deaths. At Auschwitz, by contrast, those fit enough to be used as slave labour would first be split from those, the vast majority, who were to be executed immediately. Suitcases were neatly piled, then clothes. Naked, the victims were directed towards what they were told were communal showers. Here, the doors locked, they were gassed.

ABOVE AND OPPOSITE Hungarian Jews arriving at what was known as the ramp at Auschwitz in the summer of 1944. To the left are those comparatively able-bodied men selected to serve as Sonderkommando, *to the right those – women, children, and the elderly – to be sent straight to the gas chambers.*

The Hungarian Jews

Hungary had been a German ally since October 1940. In March 1944, desperate to shore up his crumbling flanks, Hitler effectively took the country over. It was almost the last of his sudden coups. In the end, it made no difference to Hitler's war-waging capacity, but it proved wholly devastating to the country's Jews. There were almost 750,000 Jews in Hungary. Between 15 May and 9 July 1944, with the help of the Hungarian police, 437,402 of them were shipped to Auschwitz. With the war in the balance, for Eichmann such further slaughter represented a critical contribution to ultimate victory.

ABOVE The particular horror of the Holocaust was not just that it was the most obviously innocent who were killed, but that they were delivered to their places of death by exactly those mechanisms of apparent European civilization that might once have liberated them. The cattle trucks that transported the Jews to their brutal ends were a precise example of the Nazi perversion of the new world they claimed to uphold.

Amsterdam, den _6. April_ 1943.

Der niederländische Staatsangehörige _Solomon Franziska_

Zimmer 25 übergibt am _5. April 1943_

1. _M. Lopones-Rodriques, A'dam 2.5.71, Transvaalplein 10 fl_
2. _B. v. d. Poorten-de Vries, A'dam 18.4.62, Transvaalplein 29 fl_
3. _Helena Jacob, A'dam 7.2.11, Transvaalplein 20 fl_
4. _Josef de Vries, A'dam 21.8.76, Transvaalplein 20 fl_
5. _Salomon Mos, A'dam 25.5.66, Transvaalplein 19 fl._

Amsterdam.

Für die Zentralstelle für jüdische Auswanderung Amsterdam richtig übernommen: _Stern_

....
Wachhabender

_SS_-Hauptsturmführer.

1. Für die Richtigkeit der Übernahme:

2. Verwaltung

zur Zahlung von _37.50_ Gulden, in Worten _Vierund-_
dreizig, 50/100 Gulden.

Amsterdam, den _6. April_ 1943.

Festgestellt   **Sachlich richtig**

....
Polizeisekretär   _SS_-Sturmbannführer.

13 APR 1943 1943.

B. d. S.
Zahlstelle-Aussenstelle
Amsterdam

Empfangsbescheinigung:

Von der Zahlstelle des B. d. S. — Aussenstelle Amsterdam — habe ich _37.50_ Gulden,
in Worten _Vierunddreizig, 50/100_ Gulden erhalten,
Dieser Betrag ist vorschussweise aus Judenvermögen gezahlt worden.

....
(Unterschrift.)

K 372

A receipt from the SS for information received from spies about Jews in Amsterdam

The Dutch national citizen ..... [Name handwritten]
...*Room 25*...hands over on...*5 April 1943* [overwritten number 1074, underscored]
1. etc [List contains names, dates of birth and addresses of five Amsterdam residents from the same block of flats]

Amsterdam.

On behalf of the Central Office for Jewish Emigration in Amsterdam, correctly accepted by:

.... [signature] *Wolf SS Sturm*
Duty officer

1. Transfer certified correct by: [signature, illegible]
SS-Hauptsturmführer

2. Administration
for payment of 37.50 Guilders, in words ....
Thirty seven, 50/100 Guilders

Amsterdam, 6 April 1943.

Noted by
Factually correct
[signature, illegible]   [initials, illegible]
Police secretary   SS-Sturmbannführer

Commander of the Security Police   ....,
[stamp] 13 April 1943.
Payment office-field office
Amsterdam

<u>Certificate of Receipt</u>

From the payment office of the B.d.S. – Amsterdam field office, I have received ...
37.50... Guilders, in words ...*Thirty seven, 50/100* ...Guilders.

This amount has been paid by way of loan from Jewish assets.

[Signature, illegible]
(Signature)

OPPOSITE A SS receipt dated 6 April 1943 confirming that the sum of 37.5 Dutch guilders had been paid, in Amsterdam, as a loan secured against Jewish property seized from five Dutch Jews by the euphemistically named Central Office for Jewish Emigration in the Dutch capital.

Gas Chambers and Crematoria

There were five principal Nazi death camps: Chelmno, Treblinka, Sobibor, Belzec and Auschwitz, all in Poland. How they operated varied. Chelmno was always hastily improvised. Treblinka, Sobibor and Belzec were purpose built, with largely identical gas chambers and crematoria. Auschwitz, the largest and deadliest of all, was a combined labour camp and death camp. All had a common goal: the harnessing of industrial means to kill the largest number of Jews as rapidly as possible.

Working in his spare time, in 1942 Kurt Prüfer, an engineer at J. A. Topf & Sons, an engineering company specializing in crematoria, devised a method by which the heat from the crematoria already being built in the death camps could be recycled to heat the gas chambers to 26°C, the temperature at which the gas Zyklon B was most effective. His idea was readily welcomed. If his contribution to the murder of millions seems to have been motivated by little more than professional pride, his involvement highlights the extent to which the Final Solution, not just in its earliest phase (Operation Reinhard, the rounding-up and murder of Jews in Poland's General-Government), was made possible by the active co-operation of German industry on a huge scale.

Topf had first been contracted by the SS in 1939 to provide a mobile incinerator to burn the bodies of typhus victims at Buchenwald concentration camp. To an extent, whatever their expertise, Topf had partly been forestalled by the SS, whose spreading empire now embraced an architectural department. From the autumn of 1941, it had already begun drawing up meticulous plans for the expansion of Auschwitz, in the process decreeing that the emaciated Soviet prisoners who were to build it would be squeezed first 550 into a hut designed for 180, then 750, with 12 sharing a bunk intended for three.

Sonderkommando

In exactly the same way that the SS forced the Jews in the ghettos to police themselves, the labour in the death camps – above all transporting corpses to the crematoria and disposing of the remains – was carried out, on pain of instant execution, by those younger Jews deemed fit for physical work, *Sonderkommando*, literally Special Units. Though much better treated than the other inmates so as to enable them to carry out their tasks, it was a brutal business, bitterly resented by those forced into it. Every four months the *Sonderkommando* would themselves be executed and replaced with a further batch.

But this was merely laying the groundwork for the design and construction of the gas chambers and the crematoria themselves. They were built, from early 1943, two miles outside the main camp at a village called Birkenau, as replacements for the camp's original gas chambers, Bunkers 1 and 2 (*see* pages 70–71). There were eventually four crematoria at Auschwitz-Birkenau, two with gas chambers below them, with ventilation systems also supplied by Topf. Between them, crematoria II and III could dispose of 2,880 bodies a day, while crematoria IV and V could dispose of 1,536 bodies a day. In short, 4,416 corpses could be incinerated every 24 hours.

They were imposing, four-storey, brick-built affairs. They took two days to reach full working temperature. The bodies were then fed in at the top and slid downwards, ignited by those burning below them. It remained only to collect the mounting pile of ashes.

At its peak, in two months, May and June 1944, Auschwitz-Birkenau killed 264,000. This was the Final Solution transformed, a grotesque parody of industrialization, with deaths as factory targets to be met and exceeded, to be celebrated as their numbers mounted, the pitiful human cargoes disgorged by the death trains daily offering new victims. First and last, the engineers were concerned not by what the deaths meant, merely by how they could be sped up.

OPPOSITE The mockingly ironic sign over the gates at Auschwitz insisted on by the camp commandant, Rudolph Höss: Arbeit Macht Frei *(Work Will Set You Free).*

ABOVE, TOP Crematorium Four at Auschwitz-Birkenau, its lofty chimneys prominent, photographed in the spring of 1943.

ABOVE Gas ovens at Birkenau, precise products of German industrial ingenuity pressed into service on behalf of terror.

A letter from a prisoner in Auschwitz

Front

Section 1: [Two boxes]   Section 2: [Sender's address]

My address:
Name: Wantula Josef
Date of birth: 6.10.1911
Prisoner number: 32646. K4 Auschwitz, Block 13.
Post office 2.

Section 3: [Main text and address, left hand side]

Auschwitz Concentration Camp
The following rules must be observed in correspondence with prisoners:
1.) Each protective custody prisoner may receive two letters or two cards per month from relatives, and send the same to them. The letters to prisoners must be clearly legible and written in ink, and may only contain 15 lines per page. Only one standard size sheet of notepaper is permitted. Envelopes must be unlined. Only 5 x 12 pfennig stamps may be included in a letter. Anything else is forbidden and subject to confiscation. Postcards should have 10 lines. Photos may not be used as postcards.
2.) Cash may be sent.
3.) Care must be taken when sending cash or post to write the exact address on mailings, containing: Name, date of birth and prisoner number. If the address is incorrect, the mail will be returned to sender or destroyed.
4.) Newspapers are permitted, but may only be ordered through the post office of Auschwitz CC.
5.) Parcels must not be sent, as the prisoners can buy everything in the camp.
6.) It is futile to petition the camp management for the release of a prisoner from protective custody.
7.) Permission to speak to prisoners or visit them in the concentration camp will not be granted under any circumstances.

The Camp Commandant

Section 3 [address, right hand side]:

To Mrs
Broni Wantula
....
      Trzynietz O/S [Upper Silesia]
      Mozartstrasse 431. Teschen District

PRINCIPAL DEATH CAMPS

Name	Operational	Estimated minimum numbers of Jewish deaths
Auschwitz	Mar. 1942–Nov 1944	960,000
Belzec	Mar.1942–Mar 1943	450,000
Chelmno	Dec. 1941–Jan 1945	152,000
Sobibor	May. 1942–Oct 1943	180,000
Treblinka	July1942–Aug 1943	850,000

No agreed numbers for those killed exist. The most authoritative sources suggest a final death toll in the extermination camps of between 2.857 million and 3.139 million. The overwhelming majority were Jews.

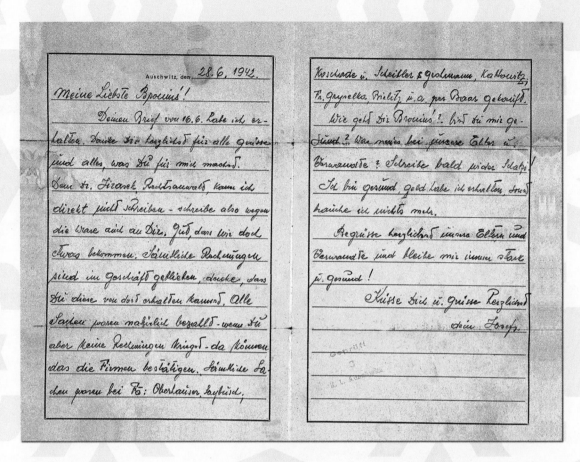

Reverse
[Left to right]

Auschwitz,

28.6.1942
My dearest Bronius!

I received your letter of 16.6. My heartfelt thanks for all the greetings and for everything you are doing for me. I cannot write directly to the lawyer, Dr Tisasek – so I am writing to you as well about the goods. Good that we are actually getting something.

All the bills were left in the shop, so I think you can get them from there. Everything was paid for, of course – if you do not get any bills, however – the companies can confirm that. Everything was with the families Oberhauser, Saybusch, Koschade and Scheibler & Geshmann, Kathowitz; Mrs Gryselka, Brielitz and others have bought through Baar.

How are you Bronius? Are you healthy? What's the news about our parents and relatives? Write again soon darling! I am healthy, I have received money, and do not need anything else.

Give our parents and relatives my warmest greetings and always stay strong and healthy for me!

With kisses and warmest greetings to you, your Josef.

THIS PAGE Selected prisoners in Auschwitz were permitted to send and receive letters, though no more than two a month. This, from a prisoner named Josef Wantula to his wife, Bronius, and dated 28 June 1942, betrays almost no sense of the horrors of the camp, concerning itself with humdrum details about his shop. It ends with "kisses and warmest greetings".

Doctors of Death

In October 1939, under what was called the T4 plan, personally ordered by Hitler, the Reich's "incurably ill" were to be given "a merciful death". The plan ended officially in August 1941, with 70,000 dead (it continued unofficially to the end of the war, killing perhaps as many as a further 200,000). Not only was gas used as a means of death for the first time, the doctors responsible asserted the programme was "entirely consistent with medical ethics".

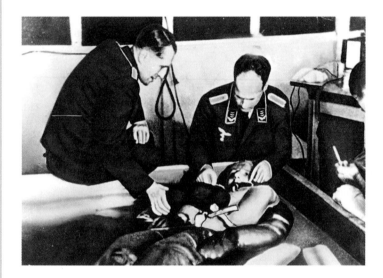

It was precisely this perversion of medical ethics that underlay one of the most disturbing features of the Final Solution: the use of Jews and other "racially inferior" types for medical experiments. As early as 1933, a compulsory sterilization programme had been introduced in Germany for the "hereditarily sick" in order to preserve the "purity" of German blood. Logic demanded its extension in 1939 to the mass euthanasia programme of the T4 plan, with women and children included for the first time. The same rationale led to its extension in April 1940 to all Jews in German mental institutions as "carriers of an infection".

If, more or less, these brutal programmes could be seen as developments of the pseudo 19th-century science of eugenics, their new application in Germany's concentration and death camps represented a radical ratcheting up of the doctrines of racial purity. Put simply, Jews and, at Auschwitz, gypsies, were to be regarded as laboratory animals, fit subjects for all and any experiments the SS deemed desirable. Their consent was not required.

The more modest of the experiments, carried out mostly in concentration camps in Germany itself, were partly concerned with the limits of human endurance, partly with human resistance to disease. The goal was to find more effective ways of aiding German forces, whether airmen forced to ditch into freezing seas or ground troops suffering gas attacks, as well as to devise better means of combatting diseases such as typhus or cholera. In all cases, the subjects were forced into a series of excruciating experiments: placed in vacuum chambers to establish how long they could survive; forced into freezing water to determine the effects of hypothermia; exposed to mustard and other poisonous gases to measure their effects, or injected with a variety of contagious diseases.

The more ambitious experiments, by contrast, were concerned much more with genetic profiles, the goal to demonstrate not merely the superiority of Aryan genetics but also the inferiority of Jewish genetics.

The most chilling figure in this most chilling of programmes was Joseph Menegle. Mengele had a double doctorate, in medicine and anthropology, from the University of Munich. In 1937, he joined the Nazi Party and, in 1938, the SS. In 1943, as a member of the concentration camp service, at his own request he was transferred to Auschwitz to undertake genetic research.

His prime interests were twins, dwarves and extreme physical disabilities. He was especially intrigued by twins with different coloured eyes and inflicted a series of operations on them in an attempt to match the colours. In almost every case, if one twin died, the other would be killed to allow a comparative post-mortem to be performed. Once, he attempted, a number of their limbs having been amputated, to sew together two gypsy twins in order to see if, forcibly conjoined, they could survive. They did not.

Whether directing his victims to the gas chambers or injecting children with diseases, he knew would kill them. Mengele, precise, polite, his clothes crisply pressed, his smile permanently ready, represented a new debasement of state-directed science.

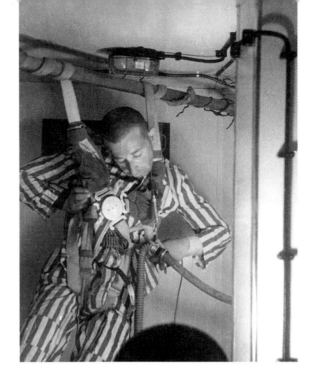

OPPOSITE A typical hypothermia experiment at Dachau, the victim forced into freezing water to discover its effect on the human body; two doctors supervise dispassionately.

OPPOSITE ABOVE RIGHT Joseph Mengele: dedicated, conscientious, deadly, as likely to give a child a sweet as a lethal injection.

LEFT The victims: gypsy children subjected to Mengele's experiments at Auschwitz.

ABOVE A Jew, incongruous in striped uniform and Luftwaffe harness, subjected to a low air-pressure experiment in Dachau. He is unconscious.

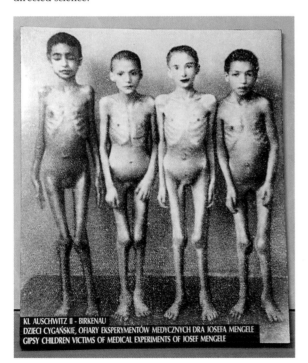

KL AUSCHWITZ II - BIRKENAU
DZIECI CYGAŃSKIE, OFIARY EKSPERYMENTÓW MEDYCZNYCH DRA JOSEFA MENGELE
GIPSY CHILDREN VICTIMS OF MEDICAL EXPERIMENTS OF JOSEF MENGELE

Mengele's Escape

In the chaos of the Third Reich's disintegration, Mengele, despite being picked up by US troops (who failed to recognize him) and subsequently travelling into the Soviet-occupied zone to gather those surviving medical records he had assembled in Auschwitz, made good his escape from Germany. In July 1949, he reached Argentina. He remained there, evading all attempts at his capture, until his death in 1979. He remains a bizarre example of Nazi terror: the disinterested man of science, apparently dedicated to the well-being of his patients (at any rate, as long as they served his purposes), who persistently subjected them to experiments that degraded and tormented them in ways that defy belief.

Slave Labourers

One of the few voices raised against the proposals for the Final Solution at the Wannsee Conference in January 1942 (see pages 50–52) was that of Erich Neumann, charged with implementing Göring's Four-Year Plan. He had no objection in principle to the slaughter of the Jews but believed they represented an obvious source of labour. Would it not make more sense for the Reich to exploit them rather than to exterminate them?

Neumann's point was not just that large numbers of Jews possessed obvious expertise in a great many fields, expertise Nazi Germany could ill afford to ignore, but that the unskilled rump could be used as slave labour. Heydrich, chairing the conference, was not swayed. In this, he precisely reflected the National-Socialist priorities of Hitler, for whom Nazi ideology always took precedence over practical considerations, however pressing. Whatever the advantages to the German war effort Jewish labour might represent, they paled when compared with the Aryan need to ensure their eradication as *Untermenschen*.

Despite most popular views of Nazi Germany as a supremely efficient war-making state, at least until 1942 – when Albert Speer was charged with its re-direction – the German economy might almost have been deliberately intended as a model of how to squander state resources in pursuit of total war. Neither centrally directed on the Soviet model nor unashamedly capitalist on the American model, it was an unhappy hybrid of competing, squabbling interests, the end result being a remarkably inefficient use of potentially immense resources.

Only belatedly was it realized that in the process an enormous pool of potential labour was being wasted. Characteristically, it was decided that if Jews and others – the net was spread very wide, to include Frenchmen, Dutch, Italians, Czechs, Hungarians, Poles, Finns, Balts, even

OPPOSITE As early as 1938, Jews were being forced into degrading manual labour. Here, a group, a number of whom are patently unfit, struggle with an agricultural cart.

ABOVE From 1943, slave labourers were used to excavate the immense tunnels where the V-1 and, later, V-2 rockets were built at the Mittelbau-Dora complex of camps near Buchenwald. Here the imposing entrance is pictured.

Germans – were to be pressed into service on behalf of the Reich, it would be as a conscripted work force: meaning, at least in the case of the Jews, slave labourers.

Whatever the advantages of a labour force that it was mostly unnecessary to feed, house or pay and whom, as they died, could be replaced by countless numbers of similar drudges, to be worked to death in their turn, it was a still an astonishingly inefficient use of them. It was, second only to the death camps, the supreme symbol of the degeneration of the decaying Nazi state, armies of dying slaves in the service of a regime whose sole goal, as its defeat became ever more certain, was an ever more fanatical determination to destroy its enemies.

If the numbers can never be known with certainty, it is presumed that by 1945 there were eight million conscripted labourers in Germany, perhaps 20 per cent of the entire German work force, with 2.4 million of them slave labourers. In 1944, in pursuit of his increasingly lurid dreams of how his *Wunderwaffen* (Wonder Weapons), the V-1 flying bomb and V-2 rocket, would bring the Allies to their knees, Hitler ordered the construction of an underground complex at

ABOVE Auschwitz was always more than a death-camp-cum-labour-camp: it was a major industrial centre. IG Farben, among Germany's largest concerns, had a synthetic rubber works here, pictured, which also produced Zyklon B.

Mittelbau-Dora where, safe from Allied bombing, they would be built. Sixty-thousand inmates of Buchenwald were despatched to construct it. Here they lived and here 20,000 died. The stench of excrement was overwhelming. It was not unusual for workers to survive for only three or four days.

Even as the Allied noose tightened, substantial numbers of Germany's largest industrial concerns increasingly came to depend on forced labour. Inevitably, those brought in from the East were subjected to the most brutal treatment. Between 1941 and 1945, 25,000 slave labourers working at the IG Farben factory at Auschwitz died.

Wunderwaffen

By late 1944, Hitler lost himself in a series of fantasies whereby his "invincible will" would ensure the sudden confounding of his enemies. An array of irresistible weapons would be unleashed: a new U-boat, the Elektroboot; the world's first jet fighter, the Messerschmidt Me 262; the Vergeltungswaffen, the vengeance weapons. That they depended on slave labour for their construction was a fitting statement of the inevitability of Aryan triumph. Yet despite leading the world in the Twenties and Thirties in nuclear research, Nazi Germany never attempted to develop the one weapon that might properly have ensured victory: a nuclear bomb. It was, Hitler claimed, "Jewish science".

ABOVE Hitler's dreams of wonder-weapons were not entirely fanciful. The Messerschmitt Me 262 was a genuinely pioneering machine, the world's first operational jet aircraft. Yet it was plagued by technical troubles, with only a handful of machines taking to the air. Even so, it instantly rendered piston-engine planes obsolete.

Der Reichsführer - ⚡

Inspekteur der Konzentrationslager   Oranienburg, den 15. Nov. 41.

   Pol./Az.: 14 f 14 /L/ Ot.-

   Geheim Tgb.-Nr.   / 41.

      Betreff: Exekution von russischen Kriegsgefangenen.
      Bezug: ohne
      Anlagen: keine

      An die
      Lagerkommandanten der
      Konzentrationslager
      Da., Sah., Bu., Mau., Flo., Neu., Au., Gr.-Ro..

      Abdr. an: Lagerärzte, Schutzhaftlagerführer (E),Verwaltungen

Der Reichsführer - ⚡ und Chef der Deutschen Polizei hat
sich grundsätzlich damit einverstanden erklärt, daß von
den in die Konzentrationslager zur Exekution überstellten
russischen Kriegsgefangenen (insbesondere Kommissare),
die auf Grund ihrer körperlichen Beschaffenheit zur Arbeit
in einem Steinbruch eingesetzt werden können, die Exekution
aufgeschoben wird. Zu dieser Maßnahme muß vorher das
Einverständnis des Chefs der Sicherheitspolizei und des SD
eingeholt werden.
Hierzu wird befohlen:
Beim Eintreffen von Exekutionstransporten in die Lager
sind die körperlich kräftigen Russen, die sich für eine
Arbeit in einem Steinbruch eignen, durch den Schutzhaft-
lagerführer (E) und dem Lagerarzt heraus zu suchen. Eine
namentliche Liste der herausgesuchten Russen ist in
Doppel ausgefertigt hier vorzulegen.

An order regarding the deployment of Russian POWs

Reichsführer SS
Concentration Camps Inspector   Oranienburg, 15 November 41
Pol./Az.: 14 f 14 /L/ Ot.-
Secret journal entry No. /41

    Subject: Execution of Russian prisoners of war
    Reference: None
    Annexes: None

    To the
    Commandants of Concentration camps   SECRET
    Da. , Sah., Bu., Mau., Flo., Neu., Au., Gr.-Ro..

Copy to: Camp doctors, protective custody camp commanders (E), administrative departments

The Reichsführer SS and Chief of German Police has agreed in principle that the execution of Russian prisoners of war (commissars in particular) transferred to concentration camps for execution, whose physical condition enables them to work in a stone quarry, should be deferred. Agreement for this measure must be obtained in advance from the Chief of Security Police and Security Service.
It is further ordered that: On arrival of execution transports in the camps, the physically strong Russians who are suitable for work in a stone quarry should be selected by the protective custody commanders (E) and the camp doctor. In this event a list of names of the selected Russians must be submitted in duplicate.

*OPPOSITE An order to selected concentration camp commandants
and marked Secret (Geheim) passing on instructions from Himmler
that physically able Russian POWs, otherwise transported for
execution, should instead be sent to work in stone quarries, in other
words as slave labourers.*

Resistance and Reprisals

One of the more curious features of the Final Solution was what, superficially, seemed a kind of co-operation on the part of the Jews in their fate. At almost no point did they offer any serious resistance to their oppressors. Even when obviously outnumbering them, they were consistently meek, almost cowering. They seemed to accept that they could be ordered to their deaths in their millions with almost no protest. On only a handful of occasions, was any serious resistance offered.

On every occasion, it was crushed with overwhelming force. Initially, recognizing their obvious powerlessness, the Jews did what they could to accommodate the Nazis: orders instantly compiled with, money raised to ransom those arbitrarily seized, volunteers put forward as hostages, police forces assembled to oppress their own people. The thinking was clear. The Jews had suffered centuries of persecution. No one in newly Nazi Germany could seriously have anticipated the horrors of Hitler's anti-Jewish crusade. Appeasement seemed the only logical way to buy time while a longer-term solution, if there was one, was found.

It fatally underestimated Hitler's savage instincts. Even as late as 1942, while the SS was planning the wholesale removal of the Warsaw ghetto to the death camps, the *Judenrat* was desperately attempting to negotiate better terms with the General-Government. They were comprehensively, contemptuously rejected.

That said, if resistance was futile, it could still be attempted. The Jews in the Warsaw ghetto had been deliberately starved, impoverished and rendered sub-human. In April 1943, those still there rose in an act of magnificent defiance in protest at the removal of almost all their numbers to their deaths at Treblinka.

Their weapons, laboriously smuggled into the ghetto at enormous risk, were pitifully few: a handful of pistols, a smaller number of rifles, a single machine gun, one land mine, a series of hand-made bombs. For four weeks, they defied every furious German effort to defeat them.

The German response was to raze the ghetto in its entirety, reducing it, building by building, street by street, by 16 May to a smouldering ruin. What was remarkable was that the Jews of the uprising knew not only that this would be the German response but also that it would mean their deaths. The survivors were counted in their dozens. They were relentlessly hunted, moving desperately from basement to basement, from sewer to sewer.

On 1 August 1944, a more sustained revolt was attempted. It was mounted not by the city's Jews but by the Polish resistance proper, the Armia Krajowa, or Home Army, significantly better armed. It presumed not just that the Soviets, poised on the outskirts of the city as they pushed towards Germany, would help them but also that the Western Allies, Britain and America, recognizing the uprising's importance, would see it as a means of speeding the defeat of Nazi Germany and restoring Polish independence.

ABOVE Perhaps the most celebrated, certainly among the most troubling images of the Holocaust, here digitally coloured. The picture was taken in late spring 1943 during the final destruction of the Warsaw ghetto and formed part of the Stroop Report, which graphically charted the destruction of the ghetto. The identity of the boy in the foreground, hands raised, remains uncertain.

The revolt was entirely crushed. Stalin was only too happy to allow the Nazis to obliterate hopes of future Polish independence, and neither Britain nor America were capable of producing more than a handful of airdrops in support of the Polish rebels, most of which anyway landed behind the Nazi lines. At almost exactly the moment that Paris was being liberated, Warsaw was being reduced to further servitude. As, later, the Nazis retreated, the Soviets advanced.

Sporadically, even in the death camps, there were still attempts to defy the Nazis. There were revolts at Treblinka on 2 August 1943; and Sobibor on 14 October 1943; and at Auschwitz-Birkenau on 7 October 1944. Yet while a handful succeeded in escaping, in all three cases the SS restored their vicious order with minimal difficulty.

ABOVE Warsaw, 8 October 1944: tattered remnants of the Polish Home Army herded through the streets of the rubble-strewn city.

The Destruction of Warsaw

When, in January 1945, the Soviet army finally entered Warsaw, a pre-war population of 1.25 million had been reduced to 174,000 stunned and starving survivors desperately subsisting in a wasteland of destruction. An estimated 600,000 had died, the rest deported. Under SS General Erich von dem Bach-Zelewski, the Germans suppressed the Warsaw Uprising with staggering ferocity, deliberately refusing to distinguish between resistance fighters and civilians: for every soldier who was killed, 1,000 civilians died. Hospitals were burned with staff and patients still inside them, women and children were chained to German tanks to prevent ambushes, insurgents covered with petrol and set alight. In a single district, Wola, up to 50,000 died.

BELOW The original title of the Stroop Report was, simply, "The Jewish Quarter of Warsaw Is No More!" It was not an exaggeration.

Death Marches

Late in 1944, as Soviet troops closed in on Germany, the SS began to move prisoners from their camps in Poland and the east of Germany to the west. In almost all cases, the prisoners walked. In bitter winter weather, a series of shuffling columns made their pitiful way back to the Reich. It was a precise symbol of Hitler's determination to sustain his disintegrating regime to the bitter end.

Even now, the chaos in northern and central Europe in the last months of the Second World War is hard to appreciate. The Soviet advance, 6.7 million men strong, was relentless and brutal. Rape, looting and wanton destruction occurred routinely. In the face of this implacably destructive force, millions of Germans, from Pomerania, Silesia and East Prussia, struggled westward over what now were not merely shattered but frozen landscapes. With the war plainly lost, they were desperate to avoid capture by the Soviets. At the same time, an estimated 80,000 Allied POWs were being deported, again on foot, to the west.

It was against this extraordinary background of terror and death, with millions uprooted, that Himmler decreed the emptying of the camps that stood in the way of the Soviet advance. His purpose was three-fold. The operation of all the SS camps had always been shrouded in secrecy: first and last, the Final Solution in particular, whatever its scale, was always to be clandestine. Yet at the end of July 1944, Soviet forces had liberated the camp at Majdanek outside Lublin in central Poland. Despite frantic last-minute efforts by the SS to empty the camp, the Soviets had discovered not only several thousand prisoners but also obvious evidence of mass murder. They made very sure the news was broadcast to the world. For Himmler, it was imperative the Allies be denied further such propaganda coups.

Second, however emaciated, in this moment of supreme crisis for the Thousand-Year Reich, the camp inmates still had some value as slave labourers. It might as well be exploited

while the inevitability of their deaths was a near given. Third, Himmler, aware of the imminence of final defeat, nonetheless nurtured the dim hope that a negotiated settlement with the Western Allies might be secured, in which case any surviving prisoners might have some value as bargaining chips.

The consequences were wholly predictable. As the prisoners began their agonizing progress to the west, they began to die. Stragglers would be beaten and, if still unable to continue, shot. Unknown numbers froze to death. One report describes the wife of an SS officer perched on a cart pulled by "six female skeletons" while she gorged on raisins.

Of the 50,000 evacuated in January 1945 from Stutthof concentration camp in northern Poland, 25,000 died. Five-thousand had previously been marched to the Baltic, forced into its frozen waters and shot. The panicked abandonment of Auschwitz, liberated by Soviet forces on 27 January 1945, saw almost 60,000 marched to a railway depot 56 km (35 miles) away. Fifteen thousand died before they reached it. Despite Himmler's stern insistence "that not a single prisoner ... falls alive into the hands of the enemy", approximately 7,500 dazed survivors were found at Auschwitz by the Soviets.

The fate of those who survived the marches was further incarceration in camps in Germany, notably Buchenwald, Dachau and Sachsenhausen. As US forces closed in on southern Germany in early April 1945, the inmates of Dachau and Buchenwald were themselves evacuated, 30,000 from Buchenwald, 7,000 from Dachau.

OPPOSITE Late April 1945: a group of prisoners from Dachau make their uncertain, halting way through the Bavarian city of Starnberg.

ABOVE An ocean of shoes photographed at Majdanek, 1945, forcibly stripped from their owners before their deaths.

BELOW On 13 April 1945, 1,000 prisoners from Mittelbau-Dora concentration camp in central Germany were evacuated before being locked in a barn and burned to death by their SS guards. Only 25 survived.

Razing the Death Camps

From the start, Hitler was determined that, the Nazi triumph assured, all traces of the death camps would be obliterated. As early as June 1943, Belzec was razed. Work began on demolishing Sobibor and Treblinka in November the same year. Inevitably, it was *Sonderkommando* – subsequently duly murdered – who were charged with the work. Yet not even Nazi ingenuity could hope to cover up so monstrous a crime. When the Soviets reached Auschwitz in January 1945, in addition to a series of twins ear-marked by Joseph Menegele for medical experiments, they found, precisely stored, hundreds of thousands of sets of clothes, men's and women's, and over seven tons of human hair.

Balkan Terror: the Ustase

The bewildering tangle of Balkan ethnic peoples and rivalries, which the creation in 1918 of the Kingdom of Serbs, Croats and Slovenes (from 1929 the Kingdom of Yugoslavia) exacerbated rather than calmed, combined in the 1930s with the elemental clash of fascism and communism to produce in a newly assertive Croatia one of the nastier fascist states. It came into being in April 1941 as the Independent State of Croatia.

In reality, it was never properly able to lay any serious claim to independence. It owed its existence to Italy and Germany, who between them, following the Italian invasion of Yugoslavia in 1941 (an invasion the Germans were then forced to bail out), exercised a loose hegemony over what from its inception was little more than a client state. Axis protection nonetheless allowed it to thrive.

The Croats considered themselves Slavs, but simultaneously saw themselves as part of a western European world. They dreamed of a Balkan state, which they would dominate, the Serbs definitively expelled. They were almost fanatically Catholic, yet they recognized Muslims as natural Croats. Above all, they defined themselves by their opposition to Serbs. It was the Serbs, Orthodox Christians, who had dominated the Kingdom of Yugoslavia and sought in the process to extinguish Croat aspirations to self-rule. A seething history of resentment and revenge, stretching over centuries, resurfaced with killing consequences.

Against this background of brutal, potentially unresolvable, ethnic tension, Croatia in 1941 emerged under the rule of Ante Pavelić as a fascist state directly modelled on Italy and Germany. The German model proved the more persuasive, a precise precedent for the extermination of its racial enemies, Serbs, gypsies and Jews.

The Ustase movement – the name meant "rise-up" or "insurgent" – had been formed by Pavelić in 1929. On 16 April 1942, only ten days after the Axis invasion of Yugoslavia, Pavelić declared it the government of an independent Croatia, though the price of Italian support was the surrender of much of its Dalmatian coast to Italy. Pavelić declared himself "Poglavnik", leader, an exact echo of the terms Duce and Führer.

Spearheaded by two élite units – the Black Legion and the Poglavnik Bodyguard Battalion – a campaign of an astounding bestiality was launched. As important, a series of concentration camps was established, of which the most notorious was Jasenovac. If it was never a death camp in the Nazi sense, it was nonetheless a place of relentless brutality in which as many as 100,000 died.

Yet almost the most notable feature of Ustase rule, desperate to project itself as a legitimate nationalist movement, was how rapidly and enthusiastically it embraced a kind of violent lawlessness that thought nothing of slaughter, that revelled in the destruction of whole villages, that prided itself on bursting into Serbian, Jewish or gypsy houses to murder all their inhabitants, that congratulated itself on hacking its victims to death, that, grinningly, sliced off women's breasts with precisely sharpened knives.

OPPOSITE Croat hostility towards the Serbs was such that even street signs in Serbian were considered a legitimate target. Here, following Croatian independence, members of the Ustase remove such a sign.

Measured against the vastly wider brutalities of the Holocaust, it is tempting to see Pavelić's Croatia as a footnote of the Second World War, a minor part of an infinitely greater crime. Yet the savagery its victims were subjected to – there is no agreed number of how many died, though 390,000 appears the most reliable estimate – would prove a potent source in fuelling the astonishing ferocity that characterized the civil wars that broke out in the 1990s as the re-constituted Yugoslavia broke apart. Short-lived or not, the Independent State of Croatia was a place of remarkable thuggishness.

Ante Pavelić (1889–1959)

Ante Pavelić was perhaps the supreme example of the minor 20th-century dictator, a lawyer who, in the name of Croat independence, was seduced by the possibilities of violently imposed nationalism. He agitated constantly against the Yugoslav government in the 1920s and 1930s, spending long periods in exile in Italy. If, following his rise to power in 1941, he recognized that it was Germany rather than Italy that would guarantee his retention of it, he nonetheless irked his German masters by his willingness to accept that Jewish Christian converts be considered Croats. He died in Madrid, after being shot, in Buenos Aires, by an agent of the Yugoslav government.

ABOVE As early as 1923, Ante Pavelić had asserted that: "The knife, the gun, and explosives are the tools with which the Croatian will regain the fruits of his labour".

LEFT A Croatian Jew, his back marked with a hastily scribbled Star of David and the letter "ž" from Židov, the Croatian for Jew.

OPPOSITE Anyone familiar with the activities of the SA in Germany, who took a particular pleasure in flaunting their aggression on the streets, would have had little difficulty in recognizing exactly the same strutting, sneering arrogance in the Ustase.

Vichy France: Quotas Exceeded

The fall of France in June 1940 marked an astonishing triumph for Hitler, accomplished against the advice of nearly his entire military establishment. Charles de Gaulle, almost the most junior member of the French government, could utter what defiance he liked from his new and enforced London exile. The facts made clear a very different truth: that conquered France had become a German satellite state with no means of liberating itself.

On 10 July 1940, a new French government, answerable to Germany and based in the spa town of Vichy in central France, was formally established. It was led by one of the most redoubtable French heroes of the First World War, Philippe Pétain. He was a man whose patriotism was unquestioned but who, pragmatically, saw accommodation with Hitler as the sole means of preserving even a token French independence. He simultaneously shared an abiding distrust of democracy and a distinct taste for authoritarian rule. Tellingly, the French Revolutionary belief in "*Liberté, Egalité, Fraternité*" was ditched in favour of the sterner virtues of "*Travail, Famille, Patrie*" ("Work, Family, Homeland").

Anti-Semitism in France had been a consistent feature of its fractured political landscape throughout the 19th century. It came to an ugly fore under the Vichy regime. As early as October 1940, the Vichy government, unprompted by Berlin, had begun to discriminate against its Jewish population under the *Statut des Juifs* (Statutes on Jews), which stripped the country's Jews of most civil rights and forbade them from holding public office, this despite the fact that in 1936 the country had elected a Jewish prime minister in Léon Blum.

They similarly did little to object when, in July 1942, the Germans began to demand that Jews in France, an estimated 350,000, be deported to Germany for "resettlement". Nonetheless, the French response to the German demands was extraordinarily accommodating: a brutal rounding-

ÉTAT FRANÇAIS

VILLE DE MARSEILLE

ARRÊTÉ

relatif au

RECENSEMENT DES JUIFS

NOUS, Préfet des Bouches-du-Rhône Administrateur Extraordinaire de la Ville de Marseille, Officier de la Légion d'Honneur :
VU la loi du 5 Avril 1884 ;
VU le décret du 20 Mars 1939, pris en exécution du décret-loi du 12 Novembre 1938 ;
VU la loi du 29 Juillet 1940 ;
VU la loi du 2 Juin 1941 ;
VU la loi du 13 Juillet 1941 ;
VU l'article 471, paragraphe 15 du Code Pénal.

.ARRÊTONS :

ARTICLE PREMIER. — Toute personne juive au regard de la loi du 2 Juin 1941 portant statut des juifs doit en faire la déclaration, sur un imprimé spécial, en l'Hôtel de Ville, service de la Police Administrative, avant le 31 Juillet 1941, délai de rigueur.
ART. 2. — La déclaration ne sera reputée accomplie que lorsque l'imprimé réglementaire aura été dûment rempli par les intéressés, et déposé, ou adressé par la poste en recommandé, à l'Hôtel de Ville. Toute déclaration effectuée avant la publication du présent arrêté ou non souscrite au moyen de l'imprimé réglementaire est nulle et de nul effet.
ART. 3. — M. le Commissaire Central de Police, M. le Commandant de Gendarmerie, M. le Directeur de la Police Administrative sont chargés, chacun en ce qui le concerne, de veiller à l'exécution du présent arrêté.

Fait à Marseille, le 22 Juillet 1941.

P. le Préfet des Bouches-du-Rhône,
Administrateur Extraordinaire de la Ville de Marseille,
Le Secrétaire Général de la Préfecture délégué :

PIERRE BARRAUD.

Imp. Municipale

up of whole families, invariably with no notice. The French authorities remained apparently unconcerned as to the eventual fates of these innocents.

If the numbers scarcely compare with those slaughtered in Eastern Europe, the suffering was no less real. In Paris alone, on 16 and 17 July 1942, French police seized more than 13,000 Jews, including 4,000 children (which the Germans had not requested), who were held in sweltering heat in a roofed-in bicycle track, the Vélodrome d'Hiver. No food was provided. There were five lavatories and one tap. After five days, they were taken by train to Auschwitz and killed.

OPPOSITE Marshal Pétain, head of Vichy France, the hero of Verdun. In the summer of 1945, he was tried for treason and sentenced to death; de Gaulle commuted the sentence to life imprisonment. Pétain died in 1951, at the age of 95, entirely senile.

ABOVE LEFT Police buses drawn up outside the Vélodrome d'Hiver, otherwise known as the Vél d'Hiv, in July 1942. They were used to transport Jews there before, according to the newspaper Paris-Midi, *they were taken to new work camps, in reality to their deaths.*

ABOVE RIGHT A poster dated 22 July 1941 instructing the Jews of Marseilles to report to the Hotel de Ville before the end of the month so that their existence as Jews could be officially recorded. Similar posters appeared across the whole of the country.

Though the Vichy government initially attempted to deport only non-French Jews – in other words, to ship back to Germany those Nazi exiles who had already sought sanctuary in France – it raised no objections when the Germans arrested French Jews. Similarly, in late August 1943, it also initiated a major round-up of French Jews in Marseilles. What help was provided to French Jews came from the *Organisation Juive de Combat*, which played a critical role in protecting Jewish families. Yet of the 75,000-plus Jews in France eventually deported to the death camps, fewer than 3,000 survived. Similarly, the hostility of the Vichy regime to the country's Jews, as epitomized by the gangs of swaggering paramilitary police it authorized, the *Milice*, made clear a disturbing identification with the most thuggish elements of Nazism.

It was a point reinforced by the fact that by 1944 France had dispatched 1.1 million young men as labourers to Germany to join the 1.3 million French prisoners of war already there. Both groups were forcibly conscripted into the ranks of Germany's slave workers.

Liberation – and épuration

The Vichy regime encompassed a great deal of ugliness. But its dying days were marked by a surge of violence that shocked and surprised even ardent anti-Vichyists. This was the épuration, or purging, of those in France deemed *collabos*, collaborators. In reality, it proved little more than an opportunity for score settling and denouncements. Women said to have slept with Germans were treated exceptionally brutally, their heads publicly shaved and swastikas stamped on their foreheads. Cocteau saw a woman "completely naked" in Paris. "They tore at her," he wrote, "they pushed her, they pulled her, they spat in her face." Recent estimates claim 9,000 deaths from executions.

LEFT Grenoble, 13 September 1944: six former members of the Milice executed by firing squad. Unlike most of the killings after the liberation of France, this at least was legal, the six having been tried before a properly constituted court.

OPPOSITE *Forged stamps. The French Resistance proved adept at producing forged identification papers bearing false stamps such as these. The most remarkable of the forgers was an Argentine-born Jew, Adolfo Kaminsky, who, from a tiny studio in Paris, produced up to 500 fake identity cards a week.*

BELOW *A postcard designed by interned Jewish children for Purim. This postcard celebrating the Jewish holiday of Purim was made by Jewish children in Camp Récébédou. The camp, in southwest France, was used to house Jews awaiting transport to Drancy outside Paris, and then to the death camps. It was in operation from February 1941 to September 1942.*

Slovakia: the Hlinka Guards

Following Hitler's final takeover of the remaining Czech lands in March 1939, an independent Slovak Republic emerged, though shorn at Hitler's insistence of Ruthenia, given in effect as a bribe to Hungary to ensure its co-operation. If to all intents and purposes little more than a German puppet and as such unashamedly fascist and nationalistic, the Slovak Republic nonetheless had a number of unusual features, not least that it was led by a Catholic priest, Jozef Tiso.

LEFT Exactly as Nazi Germany boasted the Hitler Youth, so Slovakia laid claim to the Hlinka Youth, led by one Aloyz Macek, here seen on a visit to Berlin.

OPPOSITE TOP Jozef Tiso and Adolf Hitler. From 1942, Tiso took to calling himself Vodca in direct emulation of Hitler's title as Führer.

Slovakia proved itself a model German ally, taking part in Operation Barbarossa, the invasion of the Soviet Union in June 1941, and in December that year following Hitler's lead to declare war on the United States. In late March 1942, it also acquired the unenviable reputation of becoming the first state outside Germany and German-occupied Poland to deliver Jews to the Germans for "resettlement".

There was never any doubting the extreme anti-Semitism of the Tiso regime, which almost from the moment it came into power passed a series of anti-Jewish laws, stripping Jews of basic rights, forbidding mixed marriages and banning Jews from official positions. At the same time, the Hlinka Guard, a paramilitary security force modelled on Mussolini's Blackshirts, was let loose to intimidate the country's estimated Jewish population of 89,000. The Hlinka Guard may have begun as a more or less legitimate expression of Slovak nationalism, but it rapidly became little more than a legal outlet for the thuggish tendencies of the country's criminal classes.

Even before the deportations proper began, the Slovaks had offered to send 20,000 Slovak Jews to Germany, crudely seeing this as a means of disposing of the older and feebler of its Jewish population. When the Germans refused, insisting instead that its need for forced labour demanded only younger and fitter Jews, the Slovaks compromised by offering to pay the Germans to take the Jews. A price of 500 Reichsmarks per head was agreed. Put crudely, the Slovaks were subsidizing the Germans to murder their own citizens.

Among the more distasteful aspects of the round-ups and deportations was the behaviour of the Hlinka Guards. This was more than just a matter of casual brutality, of routine beatings of the Jews in their charge, it was also the wholesale

Andrej Hlinka (1864–1938)

It is one of the more unusual features of a number of 20th-century, European, fascist regimes – in Spain and Portugal as well as in countries allied with Nazi Germany – that what the Soviet Union-dubbed "clerofascism" developed: far-right movements that defined themselves not just by nationalism but in religious terms. Slovakia remains the prime example. The Hlinka Guards, for example, took their name from Andrej Hlinka, a Catholic priest who had championed Slovakian independence well before the First World War. Like Jozef Tiso, tried and hung in 1947, for some Slovaks, even today he remains a venerated figure.

ABOVE Hlinka in August 1932. He never lived to see the independent Slovakia for which he had campaigned so persistently. He died two months before Slovakian independence, directly engineered by Hitler, was declared on 6 October 1938.

and blatant theft of their property. Money was peremptorily snatched, suitcases rifled through and valuables gleefully removed. Coats were torn from the Jews. Their footwear was stolen. Not only did many guards personally enrich themselves in the process, but they also boasted about it. As a final twist, the tiny handful of Slovak Jews who survived their imprisonment returned home to discover that their former homes had similarly been expropriated.

Over the summer of 1942, 57,000 Slovak Jews, held first in Hlinka-run camps in Slovakia, were sent by train to Poland where they were handed over to the SS. Almost all were gassed, most at Auschwitz. Though on the face of it, it seems hardly credible that the Slovak government was unaware of their fate, in the late summer of 1942 Tiso halted the deportations, claiming he had only now learned the truth. In fact, he had come under pressure from the Vatican to end his co-operation with the Germans.

It made little difference. In late 1944, determined to quell an uprising by anti-government Slovak partisans, the Slovak National Uprising, Germany moved forces to Slovakia, effectively imposing martial law. Though an estimated 6,000 Jews had already fled to Hungary, almost 25,000 remained. At least half were now rounded up by the occupying Germans and sent to their deaths.

Unlikely Heroes: the Righteous

The Israelis call them the Righteous: those non-Jews who protected Jews from the Nazis. Compared with the numbers killed, the numbers saved were scarcely a foot-note. Hardly surprisingly, it was in Poland, home to Europe's largest pre-war Jewish population, where the greatest number was saved, perhaps 150,000. But whether it was thousands or handfuls, the history of the Holocaust is studded with the stories of those who saved Jews from otherwise certain death.

ABOVE The memorial to Andrey Sheptytsky in Halych in the western Ukraine. The help Sheptytsky gave to Ukraine's Jews was unstinting. He was, it has been said, a "shining beacon of hope in the darkness".

Confronted with the implacable reality of Nazi anti-Semitism, it is no surprise if the reaction of most non-Jews, both in Germany and Nazi-occupied Europe, was to look the other way. Anyone suspected of helping Jews could expect instant execution. In Poland and the Soviet Union, their families would also be executed.

Resistance took various forms: the most effective was mounted by those with institutional means to back their defiance. The role of the Catholic church has long been a source of controversy, not least the extent to which the pope, Pius XII, may or may not have discreetly conspired in the extermination of the Jews. Yet he lobbied actively against the deportation of Hungarian Jews to the death camps in 1944. He was no less vocal in his condemnation of Jewish round-ups across Western Europe. In October 1943, when the Germans demanded that all Rome's 5,000 Jews be surrendered, almost all were given shelter in churches across the city.

Orthodox Christian communities played no less important a role. On the Greek island of Zakynthos, the Germans demanded the surrender of the island's entire Jewish community of 275. The next day, the island's bishop handed the Germans a list with two names: his and the mayor's. In the Ukraine, two brothers, Andrey Sheptytsky and Klymentiy Sheptytsky, respectively the Metropolitan Archbishop of the Ukraine and a Studite monk, hid thousands of Jews in monasteries.

A series of diplomats, frequently acting against the express instructions of their governments, also played a key role. The most successful was Carl Lutz, the Swiss vice-consul in Budapest, who on his own initiative issued exit visas to as many as 60,000 Hungarian Jews, allowing them to travel to Switzerland. No less remarkable were the activities of Chiune Sugihara, Japanese vice-consul in Lithuania, who between July and August 1940 provided 6,000 visas for Jews to travel across the Soviet Union to Japan. He had a near exact counterpart

RIGHT The Memorial of the Anonymous Rescuer in the Avenue of the Righteous at Yad Vashem, Jerusalem. It commemorates all those unknown figures who helped to preserve Jewish lives in the face of the Nazi terror.

BELOW Oskar Schindler, here seen with workers at his Enamel Factory in Kraków, Poland, was perhaps the most improbable of the Righteous, a committed Nazi whose Jewish employees he initially protected purely for commercial reasons. He subsequently went to enormous lengths, dispensing immense bribes which effectively bankrupted him, to spare them purely on humanitarian grounds. He died, in Germany, in 1974.

BELOW Raoul Wallenberg proved exceptionally resourceful in helping Hungary's beleaguered Jews in 1944–45 in the face of determined Nazi efforts to exterminate them. He routinely took extraordinary risks.

OPPOSITE Memorial to Carl Lutz in Budapest Hungary. Lutz was the Swiss vice-consul to Budapest, who issued exit visas to approximately 60,000 Hungarian Jews to enable them to travel to Switzerland.

The Danish Defiance

The pre-war Jewish population of Denmark was 7,800. The Danes, patently an Aryan race and no threat to Nazi aspirations, never numbered among the racial enemies of the Reich. Denmark's occupation by Germany after May 1940 appeared a model of co-operation between Aryan peoples. Nonetheless, on 1 October 1943, Hitler ordered that Denmark's Jewish population be deported. After hasty negotiations, the Swedes agreed to accept all Denmark's Jews. An improbable fleet of fishing boats and freighters was pressed into action. In scarcely a month, almost the entire Jewish population of Denmark had been sent across the narrow strait between the two countries to safety.

in Vienna, Ho Feng-Shan, the consul-general, who even before the war had authorized the entry into China of 1,000 Austrian Jews. Raoul Wallenberg presents a similar case, a Swedish entrepreneur who, as special envoy in Budapest in 1944, arranged for the spiriting away of an unknown number of Jews, perhaps 10,000, perhaps many more. His death at the hands of the Soviets remains a matter of uncertainty.

The most sustained opposition inevitably came in Poland itself. It was a story of individual acts of heroism in the face of relentless persecution. By the end of 1942, the Polish Council to Aid Jews, commonly known as *Zegota*, had been established under the auspices of the Home Army, the AK, not itself a notably pro-Jewish body. It was a predominantly Catholic organization, headed, unusually, by a woman, a writer, Zofia Kossak-Szczucka. It aimed particularly to protect children. The head of its children's department, Irena Sendler, a one-time nurse, saved perhaps hundreds of Jewish children, babies in particular, smuggled from the Warsaw ghetto in a variety of disguises, hidden under skirts, placed in shopping bags, wrapped as though they were loaves of bread.

CARL LUTZ SVÁJCI ALKONZUL 1895 - 1975
ÉS A CIONISTA ELLENÁLLÁSI
MOZGALOM EBBEN A HÁZBAN
ÜLDÖZÖTTEK EZREIT MENTETTE MEG
1944 - BEN

FŐVÁROSI ÖNKORMÁNYZAT
BELVÁROS - LIPÓTVÁROS ÖNKORMÁNYZATA
SVÁJCI NAGYKÖVETSÉG
CARL LUTZ ALAPÍTVÁNY

Pages from Oskar Schindler's List

K.L.Gross-Rosen-A.L. Brunnlitz /Liste d. mannl. Haftlinge,18.4.1945 Blatt 2.

Lfd. Nr.	H.Art. u.Nat.	H.Nr.	Name und Vorname.	Geburts- datum.	Beruf.
61	Ju.Po.	68886	Hartmann Salomon .	7. 5.20	Lackiergerges.
62	"	8	Grun Abraham.	14. 5.05	ang.Metallverarb.
63	"	9	Inslicht Emil.	2. 9.08	Elektrikerges.
64	"	68890	Kukurutz Salo.	24.10.13	Elektrikerges.
65	"	1	Tilles Jakob.	20.10.11	Metallverarb.
66	"	2	Wachholder Baruch.	29.11.08	Maurer.
67	"	3	Liebermann Ignacy .	16. 7.08	ang. Mechaniker.
68	"	4	Liebermann Maurycy.	27. 8.10	ang. Mechaniker.
69	"	5	Hilfstein Chaim.	14.11.86	Arzt.
70	"	6	Cajg Szmul	13. 8.20	ang. Metallverarb.
71	"	7	Haarfeiwel	1. 7.10	ang. Metallverarb.
72	"	8	Wachholder Schulim.	15. 4.03	Tischlergeh.
73	"	9	Horowitz Bernard.	28. 5.97	ang. Metallevrarb.
74	"	68901	Weinstock Josef.	6. 1.17	Tischlerges.
75	"	2	Krieger Chaskel.	8. 6.00	Schlossergeh.
76	Ju.Po.	3	Eckstein Chaskel.	14.12.08	Elektrikergeh.
77	Ju.Stls.	5	Jakubovics Kurt.	27. 7.20	Klempner u.Installat.
78	Ju.Po.	6	Lichtig Samuel.	20. 3.98	Stanzer. /Ges.
79	"	7	Silberstein Max.	21. 7.00	Bauingenieur.
80	"	8	Feldstein Wolf.	8.12.23	Eisendreher.
81	"	68911	Frankel Leon.	21. 8.05	Farbereitechniker.
82	"	2	Krantz Wilhelm.	6. 9.05	ang. Metallverarb.
83	"	3	Bleberstein Alexander.	1. 8.95	Arzt.
84	"	5	Kerner Majer.	23. 6.04	ang. Metallverarb.
85	"	6	Hallers Jakob.	15. 8.21	Tischlerges.
86	"	7	Hirsch Abraham.	28. 5.12	Stanzer.
87	"	8	Hertmann Ferdinand.	11. 8.17	Elektroges.
88	"	9	Panzer Henryk.	28.10.19	Malermeister.
89	"	68920	Weinberger Markas.	2. 3.09	Tischlerges.
90	"	1	Reisman Leon.	31.12.16	Schildermaler.
91	"	2	Oppenheim Saal.	4. 6.98	Tischlermeister.
92	"	3	Eintracht Alexander.	2. 3.06	ang. Metallarb.
93	"	5	Schneider Israel.	30. 4.12	Schreibkraft.
94	"	6	Nussubaum Wilhelm.	1. 8.10	Polsterermeister.
95	"	7	Nussubeum Richard.	22. 3.30	Lehrling.
96	"	8	Pemper Stefan.	5. 9.24	Kutscher.
97	"	9	Perl Salomon.	2. 3.07	Holzfachmann.
98	"	68930	Mutzner Jeremiasz.	25.10.10	Klempner.
99	"	1	Nichthauser Alfred.	16. 7.98	Buchhalter.
100	"	2	Posner Baruch.	17. 9.18	Maurerges.
101	"	3	Rozer Franciszok.	31.10.19	Dreherges.
102	"	4	Mindelgrun Menasche.	4. 5.17	ang. Metallverarb.
103	"	5	Muhlrad Alecksander.	9. 9.17	Wasserl.Install.Ges
104	"	6	Pemper Jakob.	30. 8.98	ang. Metallverarb.
105	"	7	Lesser Jacob.	25. 2.13	Maschinenschloseer.
106	"	8	Lesser Szulim.	5. 5.16	Schlosserges.
107	"	9	Muller Moses.	23. 5.10	Backerges.
108	"	68940	Lezerkiewicz Wiktor.	25. 8.19	Elekriker,Telefonat
109	"	1	Pechner Simon	18. 7.21	Stanzer.
110	"	2	Lewkowicz Natan.	29. 4.09	Autoschlosserges.
111	"	3	Melzer Josef.	7. 7.11	Chem. Laborant.
112	"	4	Mutzenmacher Rubin.	14.11.98	Buckermeister.
113	"	5	Lewkowicz Hermann	29. 4.09	Autoschlosser.
114	"	6	Rosenzweig Maks.	13. 4.98	ang. Schlosser.
115	"	7	Stern Henryk.	19.11.96	ang.Tischler.
116	"	8	Kleiner Bernard.	8. 5.14	Schlosser.
117	"	9	Libser Markus.	12. 3.04	Klempner.
118	"	68950	Rosenfried Albert.	24. 6.16	ang.Elektriker.
119	"	1	Reif Viktor.	24.10.00	Bauing.(Innenarch.)
120	"	68952	Nedel Dawid.	5. 6.13	Wasserinstall.Ges.

THESE PAGES
The German industrialist Oskar Schindler produced this now famous list in the summer of 1944. It detailed those Jews, almost 1,200 in all, employed by him, who, as a result of his continuous intervention on their behalf, were to be granted exemption from being sent to death camps.

112   *Unlikely Heroes: the Righteous*

Lfd. Nr.	H.Art. u. Nat.	H.Nr.	Name und Vorname.	Geburtsdatum.	Beruf.
121	Ju.Po.	68953	Glassner Henryk.	6. 1.10	Klempner/Wasserinst
122	"	4	Dosenkranz Max	25. 2.06	Schlossermeinster.
123	"	5	Neufeld Henryk.	14. 8.20	Schlosserges.
124	"	6	Horowitz Wolf.	2. 9.98	ang. Metallverarb.
125	"	7	Lewkowicz Moses.	20. 3.94	Schlossergeh.
126	"	8	Rechtschaffer Moses.	3? 3=06	Maurermeister.
127	"	9	Sellinger Chaim.	17. 7.95	ang. Tischler.
128	"	68960	Keil Josef.	12. 9.12	Klempnerges.
129	"	1	Perlmann Jakob.	31. 5.08	ang. Tischler.
130	"	2	Perlmann Chaim.	1o. 8.01	ang. Tischler.
131	"	3	Weinberger Adolf.	6. 6.10	Friseurmeister.
132	"	4	Rumpler Josef.	1. 4.98	Maler-Lack.-Meister
133	"	5	Mandel Hersch.	17.10.04	Elektregenschweiser
134	"	6	Perlmann Moses.	9.10.26	Stanzer.
135	"	7	Perlmann Hersch.	2.10.99	Riemermeister.
136	"	8	Planzer Chaim.	28. 9.01	Wasserinst.-Meister
137	"	9	Perlmann Natan.	20. 5.13	Riemerges.
138	"	68971	Wilk Sadek.	11.11.18	ang.Metallverarb.
139	"	2	Perlmann Jakow.	21. 2.09	Glaser-Lakierermst.
140	"	3	Roth Fiachel.	1912	ang.Metallverarb.
141	"	4	Schuldleher Moses.	26. 5.06	ang. Metallverarb.
142	"	5	Markeheim Maurycy.	14. 2.23	Maschinenschlosser
143	"	6	Leibler Leon.	5. 9.08	Schlosserges.
144	"	7	Hirschhorn Israel.	8.11.26	Schlosserges.
145	"	8	Opoczynski Henryk.	25.7=.24	(Schlosserges)Werkz
146	"	9	Feldmann Herman Natan.	211. 16	Stanzer.
147	"	68980	Lederer Dawid.	25. 6.07	ang. Metallverarb.
148	"	1	Mond Dawid.	16. 4.91	Metallverarb.
149	"	2	Lasser Szaja.	4= 4.11	ang. Metallverarb.
150	"	3	Loffler Hermann	17.12.14	Dreharges.
151	"	4	Lewkowicz Icek.	18. 1.17	ang. Metallverarb.
152	"	5	Lederer Mendel.	25. 8.01	Fleischermeister.
153	"	6	Lebenstein Izak.	11. 2.06	ang. Metallverarb.
154	"	7	Licht Hersch.	31. 5.06	Uhrmachermeister.
155	"	8	Katz Hermann.	2. 7.93	Schreibkraft.
156	"	9	Rabner Artur.	19. 9.18	Radiotechniker.
157	"	68990	Kurs Ignacy.	2.11.00	Tischlergeh.
158	"	1	Klipstein Isak Dawid	14. 4.95	Uhrmachermeister
159	"	2	Brandeis Josef.	19. 7.01	Optikermeister.
160	"	3	Markowski Israel.	25.11.06	ang. Metallverarb.
161	"	4	Nadel Szymon.	5. 8.08	ang. Metallverarb.
162	"	5	Szenwic Zenon.	10. 6.05	Radiotechniker.
163	"	6	Klugmann Henryk.	12.12.25	Schlosserges.
164	"	7	Linderberger Leon.	5. 1.21	Schlosserges.
165	"	8	Garfunkiel Majlech.	23. 2.22	Tischlerges.
166	"	9	Kirschenbaum Isak.	22.1-.21	Maschinenschlosserg
167	"	69000	Kirschenbaum Henryk.	16. 4.22	Schlosserges.
168	"	1	Kirschenbaum Jeremiasz	27.11.11	Schlosserges.
169	"	2	Merkrebes Juda.	28.11.21	Metallverarb.
170	"	3	Chiel Pinkas	12. 5.22	ang. Metallverarb.
171	"	4	Keller Zacharjaaz	20. 8.14	Schlosserges.
172	"	5	Kleimann Jakob.	1o. 1.12	Autoschweiser
173	"	6	Pfefferberg Leopold	20. 3.30	Schweizer
174	"	7	Murlekow Nuchyn.	12. 3.90	Kesselschmiedemstr.
175	"	8	Luftig Stefan.	17. 2.29	Metalldrehgeh.
176	"	9	Luftig Leopold.	7. 3.26	Klempnerges.
177	"	69010	Reich Jerzy.	28. 2.24	Maschinenschloserge
178	"	1	Luftig Eliasz.	17.12.95	Klemphermeister.
179	"	3	Kremsdorf Jakob.	20.11.20	Schweibermeister.
180.	"	4.	Ettinger Michal.	1o. 7.13	Schlosserges.

Nuremberg: the Trials

As the dimensions of the Final Solution became clear – that this was a crime on a scale that defied imagination, without precedent in human history – a simple question arose. Every human instinct demanded that the perpetrators be brought to justice. But what legal processes were there that could be used against those who had perpetrated it? If the guilty were to be punished, was there, properly, a legal mechanism that would allow it?

This was not an arcane legal technicality. To a huge extent, the Western allies had fought the war in defence of human freedoms and the rule of law. If those guilty of such enormous crimes were to be held to account, the means by which they were to be brought to justice must not just be legal but also be seen to be legal. Quite apart from the fact that there was no agreed global system of law – the International Court of Justice, established by what was itself a new body, the United Nations, came into being only in 1946 – it was critical that any trial be much more than a means of arbitrary justice, of victors taking their revenge on the vanquished.

There was also the problem of the Soviet Union. From 1941 onwards, the West had mounted a major propaganda exercise to portray the Soviet Union as a valiant ally, engaged, as were Britain and the United States, in a bitter struggle against a monstrous and cruel regime. Yet while it may never have sought to plunge the world into war, Stalin's Soviet Union was in every key respect as vicious and cruel as Hitler's Germany. In addition, in 1936–38, in a plain parody of legal procedures, it had mounted a series of very public show trials whose goal was quite obviously to eliminate rivals to Stalin. How could a country so ready to manipulate legality in the sole interests of its ruler conceivably play a part in what, first and last, had, legally, to be beyond suspicion?

Predictably, the answer was always a little blurred. Compromise imposed its inevitable limits. Further, the United States conducted its own trials, the last as late as 1949. Nonetheless, the most significant of the trials was the first, held in almost the only building left standing in Nuremberg, the city's Palace of Justice. Here, from 20 November 1945,

OPPOSITE The accused, November 1945. Göring, arms folded, contemptuous and resigned, is on the far left of the first row of prisoners. In front of them, wearing headphones, sit the international team of prosecutors.

ABOVE Göring, flanked by military police, takes the stand.

Albert Speer (1905–81)

Whether defiant or sullen, with one exception none of the accused at Nuremberg seemed able to understand the enormity of what they were charged with. The exception was Speer, made Armaments Minister in 1942, sentenced to 20 years' imprisonment at Nuremberg. He was cultivated, urbane, efficient and intelligent. He was an architect, charged by Hitler with the rebuilding of Berlin on a monumental scale. His time as Armaments Minister saw a huge increase in German war production, much dependent on slave labour. It seems inescapable that his acceptance of responsibility for the Nazis' crimes was an act, albeit carried off with great conviction, to escape death.

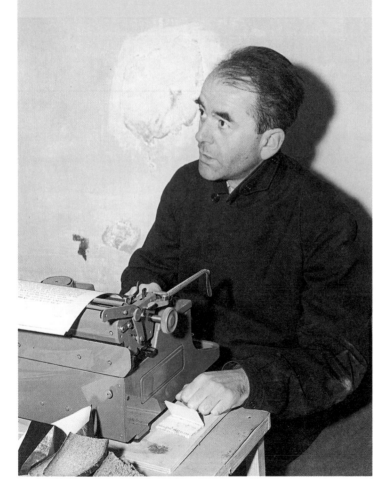

the United States, Britain, France and the Soviet Union assembled their legal teams, collectively known as the International Military Tribunal. In the dock were 24 of the most high-ranking Nazis the Allies had been able to assemble. Hitler, Himmler and Goebbels were not tried, having committed suicide as the war ended.

The United States argued, ingeniously, that the defendants were guilty of a new kind of offence: not just a determination to wage war but, in the process, of crimes against humanity. That the charge was upheld was because there was so overwhelming a need to convict those on trial. In the end, the films the court was shown of emaciated bodies being bulldozed into mass graves made the case more eloquently than any lawyer.

Of the defendants, the most impressive by far was Herman Göring. The bluff that underpinned his virtuoso performance was made exactly clear when, on 15 October 1946, the night before he was due to be executed, he was discovered dead in his cell in a pair of blue silk pyjamas having bitten a cyanide capsule.

The judges considered their verdict for over a month. There were 12 death sentences, seven imprisonments, three acquittals and two no verdicts.

LEFT Albert Speer, a little dishevelled, who in the words of journalist William Shirer, "spoke honestly and with no attempt to shirk his responsibility and his guilt", spent 20 years in Spandau prison in Berlin, many of them writing, in secret, an immense account of the Third Reich. He was released in a blaze of publicity in October 1966. He died, on a visit to London, in September 1981.

OPPOSITE Eight judges, two each from the Soviet Union, Britain, the United States and France, presided over the court, their respective flags behind them.

RIGHT Dachau liberation poster. A poster designed for a Liberation Ceremony held in Munich in May 1947 celebrating the liberation of Dachau concentration camp. The camp was still in use, holding SS members who had yet to be put on trial. Before its final closure in 1960, it was also used as a US military base.

Opening pages of the prosecution statement for the Doctors' Trial at Nuremberg

M I L I T A R Y   T R I B U N A L   N O.   I

Case No. 1

THE UNITED STATES OF AMERICA

-against-

KARL BRANDT, et al., Defendants

OPENING STATEMENT FOR

THE UNITED STATES OF AMERICA

Nürnberg
9 December, 1946

Telford Taylor
Brigadier General, USA
Chief of Counsel for War Crimes

James M. McHaney
Alexander G. Hardy
Jack W. Robbins, and
A. Herlik-Hochwald,
     of Counsel

Dr. Leo Alexander
     Medical Consultant

RIGHT AND FOLLOWING PAGES The opening pages of the prosecution statement of what is known as the Doctors' Trial, one of 12 such war crimes trials held by the US in Nuremberg. Of the 23 charged, 20 were doctors. Seven were executed, nine imprisoned, and seven acquitted.

INTRODUCTION

The defendants in this case are charged with murders, tortures,
and other atrocities committed in the name of medical science. The
victims of these crimes are numbered in the hundreds of thousands.
A handful only are still alive; a few of the survivors will appear
in this courtroom. But most of these miserable victims were slaughtered
outright or died during the course of the tortures to which they were
subjected.

For the most part they are nameless dead. To their murderers,
these wretched people were not individuals at all. They came in wholesale lots and were treated worse than animals. They were 200 Jews in
good physical condition, 50 Gypsies, 500 tubercular Poles, or 1,000
Russians. The victims of these crimes are numbered among the anonymous
millions who met death at the hands of the Nazis and whose fate is a
hideous blot on the page of modern history.

The charges against these defendants are brought in the name of
the United States of America. They are being tried by a court of
American judges. The responsibilities thus imposed upon the representatives of the United States, prosecutors and judges alike, are grave
and unusual. They are owed not only to the victims, and to the parents
and children of the victims, that just punishment be imposed on the
guilty, and not only to the defendants, that they be accorded a fair
hearing and decision. Such responsibilities are the ordinary burden of
any tribunal. Far wider are the duties which we must here fulfill.

These larger obligations run to the peoples and races on whom the
scourge of these crimes was laid. The mere punishment of the defendants,
or even of thousands of others equally guilty, can never redress the
terrible injuries which the Nazis visited upon these unfortunate peoples.
For them it is far more important that these incredible events be
established by clear and public proof, so that no one can ever doubt that
they were fact and not fable, and that this Court, as the agent of the

-2-

United States and as the voice of humanity, stamp these acts, and the ideas which engendered them, as barbarous and criminal.

We have still other responsibilities here. The defendants in the dock are charged with murder, but this is no mere murder trial. We cannot rest content when we have shown that crimes were committed and that certain persons committed them. To kill, to maim, and to torture is criminal under all modern systems of law. These defendants did not kill in hot blood, nor for personal enrichment. Some of them may be sadists, who killed and tortured for sport, but they are not all perverts. They are not ignorant men. Most of them are trained physicians and some of them are distinguished scientists. Yet these defendants, all of whom were fully able to comprehend the nature of their acts, and most of whom were exceptionally qualified to form a moral and professional judgment in this respect, are responsible for wholesale murder and unspeakably cruel tortures.

It is our deep obligation to all peoples of the world to show why and how these things happened. It is incumbent upon us to set forth with conspicuous clarity the ideas and motives which moved these defendants to treat their fellow men as less than beasts. The perverse thoughts and distorted concepts which brought about these savageries are not dead. They cannot be killed by force of arms. They must not become a spreading cancer in the breast of humanity. They must be cut out and exposed, for the reason so well stated by Mr. Justice Jackson in this courtroom a year ago:

> "The wrongs which we seek to condemn and punish have been so calculated, so malignant, and so devastating that civilization cannot tolerate their being ignored because it cannot survive their being repeated."

To the German people we owe a special responsibility in these proceedings. Under the leadership of the Nazis and the war lords, the German nation spread death and devastation throughout Europe. This the Germans now know. So, too, do they now know the consequences to Germany.

Defeat, ruin, prostration, and utter demoralization. Most German
children will never, so long as they live, see an undamaged German
city.

To what cause will these children ascribe the defeat of the German
nation and the devastation that surrounds them? Will they attribute
it to the overwhelming weight of numbers and resources that was eventually leagued against them? Will they point to the ingenuity of enemy
scientists? Will they perhaps blame their plight on strategic and
military blunders by their generals?

If the Germans embrace these reasons as the true cause of their
disaster, it will be a sad and fatal thing for Germany and for the
world. Men who have never seen a German city intact will be callous
about flattening English or American or Russian cities. They may not
even realize that they are destroying anything worthwhile, for lack of
a normal sense of values. To reestablish the greatness of Germany,
they will pin their faith on improved military techniques. Such views
will lead the Germans straight into the arms of the Prussian militarists
to whom defeat is only a glorious opportunity to start a new war game.
"Next time it will be different." We know all too well what that will
mean.

This case, and others which will be tried in this building, offer a
signal opportunity to lay before the German people the true causes of
their present misery. The walls and towers and churches of Nürnberg were,
indeed, reduced to rubble by Allied bombs, but in a deeper sense Nürnberg
has been destroyed a decade earlier, when it became the seat of the
annual Nazi Party rallies, a focal point for the moral disintegration
in Germany, and the private domain of Julius Streicher. The insane and
malignant doctrines that Nürnberg spewed forth account alike for the
crimes of these defendants and for the terrible fate of Germany under
the Third Reich.

-4-

A nation which deliberately infects itself with poison will inevitably sicken and die. These defendants and others turned Germany into an infernal combination of a lunatic asylum and a charnel house. Neither science, nor industry, nor the arts could flourish in such a foul medium. The country could not live at peace and was fatally handicapped for war. I do not think the German people have as yet any conception of how deeply the criminal folly that was Nazism bit into every phase of German life, or of how utterly ravaging the consequences were. It will be our task to make these things clear.

These are the high purposes which justify the establishment of extraordinary courts to hear and determine this case and others of comparable importance. That murder should be punished goes without the saying, but the full performance of our task requires far more than the just sentencing of these defendants. Their crimes were the inevitable result of the sinister doctrines which they espoused, and these same doctrines sealed the fate of Germany, shattered Europe, and left the world in ferment. Wherever those doctrines may emerge and prevail, the same terrible consequences will follow. That is why a bold and lucid consummation of these proceedings is of vital importance to all nations. That is why the United States has constituted this Tribunal.

Israel: Birth of a Nation

On 29 November 1947, the United Nations agreed the formation of an Israeli state in Palestine, then under British rule. If the vote was the result of intense lobbying by the United States, it nonetheless reflected clear political realities: not just that Britain was desperate to divest itself of colonial territories it could no longer sustain but also that Jewish sufferings at the hands of the Nazis demanded the Jews be accorded a state of their own.

The State of Israel, proclaimed at midnight on 14 May 1948, sparked jubilant celebrations in the infant nation that hours later were followed by the invasion of five Arab armies. A month of bitter fighting followed before the first of a series of UN-brokered ceasefires was negotiated. When the war ended on 10 March 1949, the Arab forces, poorly led, poorly armed and divided among themselves, had been routed.

The creation of the Israeli state was – as it remains – a paradox. On the one hand, it was an act of extraordinary and energetic nation-building in the face of daunting odds, a determination to celebrate the survival of world Jewry as much as to commemorate those millions who had died in the Holocaust. It promised a Jewish homeland after 2,000 years of persecution and the seemingly permanent scattering of the Jews, the diaspora. It simultaneously transformed an impoverished region of the Middle East, whatever its immense historical and religious significance, into a thriving modern state. It remains the only democracy in the Middle East.

On the other hand, this exceptionally vibrant state was created at the obvious cost to the Arab peoples of Palestine. An estimated 700,000 Palestinian refugees were forced to flee their homelands. Their numbers vastly swollen today, their fate remains as unresolved as it was in 1949. It similarly sparked a series of further Arab–Israeli conflicts – in 1956, 1967, 1973 and 1982 – as well as periodic spasms of violence in which the victims have been civilians on both sides.

It remains one of the great destabilizing factors in the world. It was a major focus of Cold War hostility just as it has since become a prime target of militant Islam. All attempts at lasting peace settlements have failed, whatever the initial promise of some and, on occasion, the obvious good will on both sides. Increasingly, it has

---

OPPOSITE Ships, many distinctly elderly, crowded with Jewish refugees anxious to reach Palestine were routinely turned away by the British, only too uncomfortably aware that further influxes of Jewish settlers would inflame the instability of Palestine.

ABOVE Israeli troops advance against Egyptian forces in the Negev in the 1948–9 Arab-Israeli war. Israel's eventual victory may have owed much to US support. Ultimately, it stemmed from exceptionally high levels of motivation and organization. By contrast, the Arab armies, Jordan's excepted, were poorly trained, badly led and frequently apathetic.

become an object of hostility for precisely those *bien-pensant*, left-leaning liberals in the West who initially were among its most enthusiastic supporters.

At heart, the problem has never really changed. From the start, the 19th-century movement that culminated in the creation of Israel – Zionism – was confronted by inescapable political realities. Initially, this was Ottoman rule of Palestine. From the end of the First World War, it was British rule, though one compromised by a series of contradictory promises to Arabs and Jews alike. By the 1930s, the consequence was an escalation of violence on both sides. The initial British reaction was to re-impose order by whatever means necessary; by 1947, it was to abandon both parties in the hopes of making as early a departure as it could decently contrive. As the British pulled out, a cornucopia of American aid – military, financial and political – ensured not just Israel's initial survival but also its continued survival.

Israel was a state founded on the highest moral principals, of justice, of fairness, of opportunity, of refuge, dedicated to righting millennia of obvious wrongs and persecution. A resolution of its enduring problems with the Arab world remains elusive.

Theodor Herzl (1860–1904)

In 1897, in the Swiss city of Basel, the first World Zionist Conference was held. It was the brainchild of an Austrian-Jewish journalist, Theodor Herzl. Zionism grew from a desire to provide the Jews with a permanent homeland of their own and to protect them from the pogroms and persecutions of late 19th-century Russia, then home to the overwhelming majority of the world's Jews. Articulate, determined, well connected, a series of its representatives subsequently launched a remarkable assault on world opinion, crucially swaying opinion in Britain and the United States. It spawned two equally impressive figures, Chaim Weizmann, the first president of Israel, and David Ben-Gurion, its first prime minister.

ABOVE Theodor Herzl, visionary and founding father of the Zionist movement. "Zion" itself is the Hebrew for "Jerusalem".

OPPOSITE BOTTOM *David Ben-Gurion, who would become Israel's first prime minister, reads the Declaration of Independence on 14 May 1948 in Tel Aviv, during a ceremony founding the State of Israel.*

LEFT Young Jews from Poland, Latvia and Hungary hold a flag bearing the Star of David from the window of a train en route to Palestine after being released from the Buchenwald concentration camp, June 1945.

Survivors

Far from rejoicing at their salvation, the handful of people who survived the Holocaust found themselves haunted and dislocated. The dominant emotion was guilt. Why had they lived when so many had died? Simultaneously, they had to confront the knowledge that, almost without exception, their families had been exterminated. In addition to the deprivations they endured, they were tormented by the horrors they witnessed. How were they to make sense of the world again?

In almost every case, the armies of starved, scarcely human wrecks that the Allies discovered at the end of the war were unable to talk about what they had suffered. Given that almost all were close to death, with even the healthiest glassy-eyed and uncomprehending, this hardly seemed surprising. More tellingly, as, painfully, they attempted to rebuild their lives, they remained silent. In effect, they had been paralyzed, almost stupefied, rendered incoherent by the scale of the suffering to which they had been subjected.

Little by little, the survivors rediscovered themselves. It was an agonizing process. A tiny, illuminating detail is provided by Irene Zisblatt, an Hungarian Jew, deported with her entire family to Auschwitz in the summer of 1944. Still in her teens, she was, apparently, one of the lucky ones, detailed to work as a slave labourer at the camp.

As such, by chance, she saw a series of trucks draw up. Two emaciated children fell from one of them. An SS guard threw them back on, having first smashed one against the back of the truck. In her own words: "That's when I stopped talking to God". Her own family had already been murdered.

A no less excruciating testimony is provided by another Hungarian Jew, Renée Firestone. Her family was given half an hour to leave their home. Determined to preserve only happy memories, she chose and put on a bathing suit given to her by her father. After a five-day journey in a cattle-car to

Auschwitz, she was ordered to strip for a shower. She was still wearing the bathing suit. She recognized that taking it off, as she did, would effectively sunder every link with her former life. She subsequently saw her father for the last time, gaunt and shaven headed, being led away in a work detail. As he, in turn, saw her, tears rolled down his face.

Given these horrors, the questions that arose for the survivors were how their own lives could be reconstructed and whether any form of understanding, of resolution, with

ABOVE US troops and camp inmates mix at Buchenwald. The American journalist Edward Murrow visited the camp the day after its liberation. "The stink," he wrote, "was beyond all description."

OPPOSITE Among the most eloquent of the survivors of the Holocaust was the Hungarian-born Tom Lantos, one of thousands sheltered by Raoul Wallenberg in Budapest. He emigrated to the US in 1947. From 1980 to his death in 2008 he served, as a Democrat, in Congress. He was an unflinching champion of human rights.

Primo Levi (1919–87)

Perhaps the most articulate and anguished voice of any Holocaust survivor was that of the Italian, Primo Levi, incarcerated in Auschwitz between February 1944 and January 1945. He consistently returned to the same point: how could the Germans have stood by while so monstrous a crime was perpetrated? If the Germans could allow themselves to be debased in this way, surely any people could. He never blamed the Germans. But he never forgave them, consistently aware, the precedent set, that others might imitate them. His tortured recognition that humans were capable of evil on such an immense scale led to his suicide in 1987.

ABOVE Primo Levi, his tattooed Auschwitz prisoner number still visible on his left forearm.

RIGHT Prisoners at Buchenwald, liberated by troops of the US Third Army on 11 April 1945. It was the first camp the Americans reached. The global impact of the discovery of these "living corpses" – 21,000 were liberated in total – was immediate and devastating.

what they had suffered was possible. If it could never be made sense of, could they at least come to terms with it, to accept it for what it was? The answers were, and continue to be, patchy.

Even 60 or 70 years after the fact, visits to the death camps by those who survived them have proved extraordinarily traumatic experiences. There is similarly the question of whether any kind of forgiveness can be extended by the survivors towards those Germans who fought in the war.

In most cases, Holocaust survivors, survivors perhaps because they possessed the moral courage to endure against impossible odds, have rebuilt their lives. As they age, they can boast of grandchildren, they can dream of future generations. Yet they are simultaneously obliged to remember other lives, no less vivid, no less real, lives they were once themselves a vital part of, which were deliberately obliterated. It remains a burden that may be endured but can never be lifted.

State Terror Continued

The scale of the Final Solution was such – given its all encompassing enormity and its startling cruelty – as to give it a uniquely evil status, a crime beyond all others before or since. Yet while it may be true that no other regime has attempted to exterminate an entire people simply on the basis of their supposed racial inferiority, it is the case that terror has underpinned a depressingly large numbers of states.

Tyranny may be a constant of human history, but at the very minimum it is arguable that state terror, organized and deliberately directed, is one of the defining characteristics of the 20th century and beyond. If nothing else, the numbers of those oppressed, tortured, starved and murdered effortlessly exceed those of any other period. If in general it declined after 1945, at least in the Western world, it thrived elsewhere, in Asia above all.

None of which is to suggest that the Holocaust was merely one part of this woeful pattern, not least because it remains the only such slaughter whose prime perpetrator simultaneously unleashed a global war that became by some distance the largest event in the history of humanity. It is worth making the point, too, that the Final Solution itself was compressed into less than three years. The sheer concentration of Nazi atrocities remains horrifying.

With that said, the most immediate parallel in the same era to Nazi Germany was provided by the Soviet Union under Joseph Stalin. Even today, the scale of the atrocities committed under Stalin remain relatively little known. Yet estimates of deaths directly attributable to him vary from 20 million to 60 million. Even if the lower figure is accurate, which most scholars doubt, that still means that during his 30-year rule an average of at least 650,000 were killed by him every year. Furthermore, after 1945, he progressively imposed on those Eastern European countries liberated by the Soviets a grimly totalitarian communist rule that enslaved millions and endured a further 36 years after his death in 1953.

The American political scientist, R. J. Rummel, coined the term "democide" to describe what he called "the murder

---

ABOVE Russian peasants in Kiev, 1934. Arguably Stalin's deliberate starvation of vast numbers of Soviet citizens – the Holodomor – was no more than a continuation of the instinctive brutality of Romanov Russia. In reality, it marked a new level of deliberate state terror.

of any person or people by a government". The term was derived from "genocide", itself coined only in 1944 by a Polish Jew, Ralph Lemkin, in response to the Final Solution. Just as genocide is hybrid word, derived from the Greek "*geno*", meaning race, and the Latin "*cide*", meaning kill, so democide is derived from "*demos*", the Greek for state. Rummel estimates the total number of the victims of 20th-century democide as 169 million. It is a figure that dwarfs the number of all those killed in the 20th century's wars.

It is important not to lose sight of the extraordinary brutality that is an invariable element in all such democides. At least 8 million died in the Congo Free State between 1886 and 1908, a country that was the personal property of the Belgian king, Leopold II. The Ottoman Turks massacred over 1 million Armenians in the First World War. In just three years, 1976–79, Pol Pot was responsible for as many as 3 million deaths in Cambodia, perhaps a quarter of Cambodia's entire population. "Ethnic cleansing" in Bosnia after 1992 – genocide by any other name – reintroduced into Europe the kind of barbarism most presumed the defeat of Hitler had ended for good. While, in only three months in 1994, perhaps 1 million Tutsi people were murdered by Hutu in Rwanda. State-sponsored brutality remains a depressingly central feature of humanity.

The Gulag

The Soviet Union may never have boasted the death camps of the Nazis, but in the Gulag, a series of penal settlements and labour camps scattered across the country, it possessed a more or less direct parallel with Nazi Germany's concentration camps. Tsarist Russia had had little compunction in sending anyone identified as a political opponent to such camps; communist Russia, above all under Stalin, greatly expanded the system. Not only the victims of Stalin's purges were incarcerated, invariably without trial. Non-Russians, Poles and Balts in particular, deemed a threat to Soviet security were also particular targets. The camps were scaled down after Stalin's death but the system endured until the 1980s.

ABOVE TOP Potocari Memorial Cemetery, Srebrenica, Bosnia and Herzegovina, 11 July 2011: a Bosnian-Muslim women weeping over one of the 613 coffins buried that day to join the 4,524 victims already interred there. All were killed in July 1995 by Bosnian Serbs commanded by Ratko Mladić. The 16-year delay in their burial was the result of the need to identify each of the bodies. In all, 8,372 were slaughtered.

ABOVE Approximately 63,000 Tutsi fled Rwanda to neighbouring Burundi as the Hutus began their indiscriminate massacres of the Tutsi in April 1994. The resulting refugee camps were places of predictable squalor.

Where was God? Men vs Monsters

The most disturbing feature of the Holocaust was not that it was the work of monsters, though Nazi Germany had more than its fair share, but that it was the work of the perfectly ordinary, those who collectively seemed to have suspended all vestiges of common humanity in the interests of mass murder. They were people who allowed themselves to commit acts of barbarity that in any other circumstance would have appalled them.

A variety of reasons have been put forward to explain how the otherwise sane and seemingly reasonable – women as well as men – could have been complicit in so staggering a crime, one which almost by definition demanded the suspension of all instinctive regard and fellow-feeling for other humans: that they were following orders; that they operated in a culture of permanent threat and fear; that they presumed it their patriotic duty; that they were unaware of what they doing.

None really convinces. The point was always that while the Final Solution may never have been possible without Hitler, it nonetheless involved – in fact demanded – the active co-operation not just of soldiers but also of civilians: railway workers, factory hands, industrialists, doctors, lawyers, policemen, civil servants. And it was a co-operation willingly given. Whatever their subsequent shocked protestations that they had no idea of what it all meant, they were irredeemably complicit. They were all party to a vast crime.

OPPOSITE Ordinary lives, extraordinary deaths: the innocent murdered not for anything they had done but simply because of who they were.

ABOVE The Eternal Flame in the Hall of Remembrance at Yad Vashem in Jerusalem. In front of it is a grave containing ashes of Holocaust victims. The names of 22 of the Nazis' principal killing sites, not just death camps and concentration camps but the likes of Babi Yar, are on the floor. The building was opened in 1961.

The lesson it reveals is deeply troubling. It is one reinforced by similar state killings in all parts of the globe, even if none was performed with quite the same ferocious zeal as the Holocaust. It is not just that ordinary people in extraordinary circumstances are capable of exceptional cruelty but also that they become inured to them. Murder becomes normal, routine, expected, everyday, unremarkable. The sufferings of others become immaterial, taken for granted.

Whatever the historical curiosities that had allowed as strange and shattered a personality as Hitler to dominate Germany after 1933, whatever the legacy of the First World War, whatever the apparently terminal failures of democracy and capitalism in the 1930s, whatever the elemental, Darwinian struggle for supremacy that then seemed inevitable between communism and fascism, the key point can never be dodged. A civilized people allowed itself to become party to a regime that committed the most monstrous crime the world had ever seen. The best that can be said of most Germans is that they were unwilling accomplices in Hitler and Himmler's atrocities. Nothing can disguise the much more uncomfortable truth that they were eager participants.

Since 1945, German contrition has been absolute. Painfully reconstructed, Germany, conjoined with its former enemies, played a key part in launching Europe on an unprecedented period of peace and prosperity, further underlined with the collapse of communism in 1989 and the unification of its sundered halves. The great ideological battles of the 1930s, which had plunged the world into war, had plainly been routed. Democracy and capitalism had no less plainly triumphed.

Yet the prospect of another descent into barbarism can never be discounted. If history teaches anything, it is that civilization is fragile; that liberties are easier to lose than to win; that freedoms need always to be guarded; that democracy is far from a natural state. And lurking under all these painful truths is that ordinary humans possess an extraordinary capacity for bestiality.

The cry that resonated as millions of Jews were put to death in the Final Solution was "Where was God?" William Styron answered it precisely: "Where was man?"

OPPOSITE Survivor and former Auschwitz camp inmate, Renee Firestone, visits a memorial in Los Angeles, during a Yom HaShoah commemoration event, which honours the memories of the victims and survivors of the Holocaust, 28 April 2019.

BELOW A memorial ceremony takes place at the Stone Flower monument on 12 April 2018 for the tens of thousands who were killed in the extermination camp at Jasenovac. The camp was set up in mid-1941 by Croatia's Ustase regime.

Further Information

Suggested Reading

Ainsztein, R, *Jewish Resistance in Nazi-Occupied Eastern Europe* (New York, 1974)

Arendt, Hannah, *The Origins of Totalitarianism* (New York, 1966)

Arendt, Hannah, *Eichmann in Jerusalem: A Report on the Banality of Evil* (New York, 1963)

Bartov, Omar, *The Eastern Front 1941–45: German Troops and the Barbarisation of Warfare* (London, 1985)

Bessel, R, *Political Violence and the Rise of Nazism: The Stormtroopers in Eastern Germany 1925–1934* (London, 1984)

Bosworth, R J, *Explaining Auschwitz and the Holocaust: History Writing on the Second World War* (London, 1973)

Broszat, M et al, *Anatomy of the SS State* (London, 1968)

Braham, R, *The Politics of Genocide: The Holocaust in Hungary* (2 vols., New York, 1981)

Bramsted, E K, *Goebbels and National Socialist Propaganda 1925–45* (London, 1965)

Breitman, Richard, *The Architect of Genocide: Himmler and the Final Solution* (New York, 1991)

Browning, Christopher, *Fateful Months: Essays on the Emergence of the Final Solution* (New York, 1985)

Browning, Christopher, *Ordinary Men: Reserve Police Battalion 101 and the Final Solution in Poland* (New York, 1992)

Browning, Christopher, *The Origins of the Final Solution: The Evolution of Nazi Jewish Policy 1939–1942* (London, 2005)

Browning, Christopher, *The Path to Genocide* (Cambridge, 1992)

Bullock, Allan, *Hitler: A Study in Tyranny* (London, 1964)

Bullock, Alan, *Hitler and Stalin Parallel Lives* (London, 1991)

Carell, P, *Hitler's War on Russia* (2 vols., London, 1970)

Cesarani, D, *The Final Solution: Origins and Implementation* (London, 1994)

Cohn, Norman, *Warrant for Genocide* (London, 1967)

Conway, J, *The Nazi Persecution of the Churches* (London, 1968)

Dawidowicz, Lucy, *The War Against the Jews* (London, 1975)

Delarue, J, *The History of the Gestapo* (London, 1964)

Fleming, Gerald, *Hitler and the Final Solution* (London, 1985)

Fromm, Erich, *The Anatomy of Human Destructiveness* (London, 1977)

Gilbert, Martin, *Atlas of the Holocaust* (London, 1982)

Gilbert, Martin, *The Holocaust: The Jewish Tragedy* (London, 1986)

Gilbert, Martin, *The Holocaust* (London, 1989)

Gordon, Sarah, *Hitler, Germans and the "'Jewish Question"* (Princeton, 1972)

Hayes, P, *Industry and Ideology: IG Farben in the Nazi Era* (Cambridge, 1987)

Hilberg, R, *The Destruction of the European Jews* (3 vols., New York, 1985)

Hirschfeld, G, *The Politics of Genocide: Jews and Soviet Prisoners of War in Nazi Germany* (London, 1986)

Homze, E L, *Foreign Labour in Nazi Germany* (Princeton, 1967)

Kershaw, Ian, *Hitler, the Germans and the Final Solution* (New York, 2009)

Kogan, E, *The Theory and Practice of Hell: The German Concentration Camps* (New York, 1950)

Laqueur, W, *The Terrible Secret* (London, 1980)

Levi, P, *If This is a Man* (London 1960)

Levi, P, *The Drowned and the Saved* (London, 1988)

Lifton,Robert, *The Nazi Doctors* (New York, 1986)

Longerich, Peter, *Holocaust: The Nazi Persecution and Murder of the Jews* (London, 2012)

Maier, Charles, *The Unmasterable Past: History, Holocaust and German National Identity* (Cambridge, MA, 1988)

Muller, Filip, *Eyewitness Auschwitz: Three Years in the Gas Chamber* (London 1999)

Marrus, M R, and Paxton, R O, *Vichy France and the Jews* (London, 1981)

Marrus, M R, *The Holocaust in History* (Hanover, NH, 1987)

Moorehead, Caroline, *Village of Secrets: Defying the Nazis in Vichy France* (London, 2014)

Neville, Peter, *The Holocaust* (Cambridge 1999)

Overy, Richard, *War and Economy in the Third Reich* (London,1994)

Overy, Richard, *The Dictators: Hitler's Germany and Stalin's Russia* (London, 2004)

Rees, Laurence, *Auschwitz: The Nazis and the Final Solution* (London, 2005)

Reitlinger, G, *The Final Solution* (London, 1953)

Roseman, Mark, *The Villa, the Lake, the Meeting: Wannsee and the Final Solution* (London, 2003)

Schleunes, K, *The Twisted Road to Auschwitz: Nazi Policy Towards German Jews 1933–39* (Urbana 1970)

Sereny, Gitta, *Albert Speer: His Battle with Truth* (London, 1995)

Smith, L, *Forgotten Voices of the Holocaust: True Stories of Survival From Men, Women and Children Who Were There* (London, 2006)

Speer, A, *Inside the Third Reich* (London, 1970)

Speer, A, *The Slave State: Heinrich Himmler's Masterplan for SS Supremacy* (London, 1981)

Stein, G H, *The Waffen SS: Hitler's Elite Guard at War 1939–45* (Ithaca, 1966)

Steinberg, Jonathan, *All or Nothing: The Axis and the Holocaust 1941–43* (London, 1990)

Sydnor, C, *Soldiers of Destruction: The SS Death's Head Division 1933–1945* (Princeton, 1977)

Taylor, T, *The Anatomy of the Nuremberg Trials* (London, 1992)

Trunk, Israel, *Judenrat* (New York, 1972)

Wyman, D S, *The Abandonment of the Jews: America and the Holocaust* (New York, 1984)

Zullo, Alan, and Bovsun, Mara, *Survivors: True Stories of Children in the Holocaust* (London, 2005)

Websites

Jewish Virtual Library
jewishvirtuallibrary.org

United States Holocaust Memorial Museum
ushmm.org

Yad Vashem
yadvashem.org

ABOVE *A survivor pays tribute at the Death Wall in Auschwitz Museum,*
27 January 2019.

Index

Page numbers in *italics* refer to
photographs and documents, those in
bold refer to entire chapters.

RIGHT Gaunt survivors grip the barbed-wire fence during their liberation from the Buchenwald camp by US forces.

Credits

The publishers would like to thank the following sources for their kind permission to reproduce the photographs in this book.

Key: t = top, b = bottom, l = left, r = right & c = centre

Akg-Images: 19, 26-31, 36, 39 (b), 41 (t), 45 (t), 50, 69, 72-73, 75, 76, 80, 82, 83, 87, 88, 89, 96, 97 (b), 109 (t), 109 (b), 134

Alamy: CTK: 106 (l); /Steve Allen Travel Photography 81 (b); /V.Dorosz 111; /Eddie Gerald 135; /Viktor Onyshchenko 109 (b)

Bridgeman Images: 25

DPA: Berliner Verlag/Archiv 45 (b)

Getty Images: 40 (b), 41 (b), 112-113, 142-143; /Bentley Archive/Popperfoto 114; /Bettmann 129; /GPO 126 (b); /Heinrich Hoffmann/ullstein bild 13; /Hulton Archive 132; /Imagno 18, 33; /Keystone/Hulton Archive 12, 101 (r); /Fred Ramage 4; /FPG/Hulton Archive 20-21; /Hulton Archive 86, 116; /Imago 126 (t); /Andrej Isakovic/AFP 133 (t); /Keystone 125; /Zoltan Kluger/GPO 124; /LAPI/Roger Viollet 102; /Denis Lovrovic/AFP 137; /Tatyana Makeyeva 128; /Mondadori Portfolio 130; /OFF/AFP 22; /Mark Ralston/AFP 136; /Patrick Robert/Sygma/CORBIS/Sygma 133 (b); /Roger Viollet 89, 101 (l); /Sovfoto/Universal Images Group 44 (b), 46; /Time Life Pictures/National Archives/The LIFE Picture Collection 17; /Topical Press Agency 15; /Universal History Archive 16, 32; /US Army 127; /Alexander Vorontsov/

Galerie Bilderwelt 2-3; /Beata Zawrzel/NurPhoto 9, 139

Historical & Special Collections, Harvard Law School Library: 119-123

PA Images: 38, 39, 43 (t), 104 (b),

Photo Scala, Florence: bpk, Bildagentur fuer Kunst, Kultur und Geschichte, Berlin 11, 14, 24, 44 (t), 68

Mary Evans Picture Library: 53-67, 118

Mémorial de la Shoah: 6-7, 104 (t), 105

NARA: 130-131

Private Collection: 71

Topfoto: 40 (t), 77, 78, 79, 81 (t), 84 (t), 85 (t), 94, 107 (r), 110; /Granger, NYC 48; /Roger-Viollet 47, 74, 95, 103 (l), 103 (r); /Sputnik 42, 43 (b); /Ullstein bild 23; 52, 70, 85 (t), 92-93, 97 (t), 99, 101, 106, 115, 117; /World History Archive 49, 51, 84 (b)

U.S. Holocaust Memorial Museum: Family in the ghetto, Halina Olomucki 36-37

Every effort has been made to acknowledge correctly and contact the source and/or copyright holder of each picture and the Welbeck Publishing Group apologises for any unintentional errors or omissions, which will be corrected in future editions of this book.